F

Smart Money Management

PREPARED BY THE

J. K. Lasser Tax Institute

A FIRESIDE BOOK
Published by Simon and Schuster
New York

Designed by Irving Perkins Associates
Manufactured in the United States of America
1 2 3 4 5 6 7 8 9 10

Library of Congress Cataloging in Publication Data
ISBN: 0-671-45979-1

PREFACE

INFLATION and fluctuating interest rates have shaped the American economy since the late 1970s. Now more than ever, it is important to get the most for your money and invest wisely. *J. K. Lasser's Smart Money Management* can help you develop a personalized program to control your finances.

Designed for use by singles and married couples, young people starting out, and persons about to retire, it offers methods, advice, and suggestions for managing your personal finances. This comprehensive book includes information on investing your money for the best return in today's market, as well as planning for your long-range goals. Your application of the ideas presented here may enable you to resolve current financial difficulties and to meet future financial challenges. *Smart Money Management* is a thorough, concise guide everyone can use to plan for a lifetime of financial security.

We gratefully acknowledge the contributions of Helen O'Donnell, Joyce Clarke, and Linda L. Seymour; and Elliott Eiss and Barbara E. Weltman, members of the New York Bar.

Bernard Greisman,
Director
J. K. Lasser Tax Institute

CONTENTS

8. YOUR LIFE INSURANCE PROGRAM 156

9. PERSONAL LIABILITY INSURANCE 175

10. FINANCING A COLLEGE EDUCATION 189

11. PLANNING FOR YOUR RETIREMENT 203

12. PLANNING YOUR ESTATE 225

Chapter 1

YOUR FINANCIAL PROGRAM

FOR many people, financial security is a goal which they hope will come automatically when they reach a certain income level. However, earning more does not guarantee financial security in this age of inflation and high taxes. While the median income in the United States rose from $9,867 in 1970 to $21,023 in 1980, inflation and personal income taxes erased almost all the gain. The answer then lies not just in earning more money, but in managing what you have made.

Your employment, location, family situation, lifestyle, and goals will determine your earnings and your expenses. According to a Labor Department survey, moderate living costs for a family of four in 1981 totaled $23,273 in Atlanta, $25,358 in Chicago, $29,540 in New York City, and $25,025 in Los Angeles. The Labor Department estimated that a four-member family would require at least $15,323 just to get by.

At the moderate level, the greatest expenses for a four-member family are contributions to Social Security and personal income taxes. Food is the next major expense, taking 23% of the budget, followed by housing with 21.8%. The percentage devoted to housing varies greatly. A renter may pay

11

less; a new homeowner usually pays more. The national average for annual payments on new mortgages is 33% of household income. In some cities, such as San Diego, the average percentage climbs to over 40%.

Figures for single households, which now make up more of the American population than ever before, will vary greatly from family averages. Generally, for singles, more income goes to housing but less to food.

Below is a table of how Americans, on average, spend their income after taxes and savings, according to the U.S. Department of Commerce:

ITEMS	PERCENTAGE
Food and beverages	*20.6%*
Home consumption	13.3
Dining out	4.8
Alcoholic beverages	2.5
Housing	*16.5*
Transportation	*14.1*
Purchase of cars and other vehicles	4.2
Operation and maintenance costs	8.7
Public transportation	1.2
Household expenses	*13.7*
Furnishings and appliances	2.1
Utilities	6.8
Other	4.8
Medical care	*10.4*
Clothing and jewelry	*7.4*
Recreation	*6.3*
Personal business	*5.3*
Private education	*1.5*
Philanthropy	*1.4*
Personal care	*1.4*
Tobacco	*1.2*
Other	*.2*
	100%

Budgeting your income

Budgeting is the careful allocation of your income to all expenses, requiring diligent record keeping to enable you to meet your obligations and fulfill your goals. It is not an easy task. Spending decisions must be made. Record keeping is a constant and sometimes tedious job. Analysis of income and expenses requires realistic acceptance of your circumstances. The difficulty of budgeting is evidenced by Congress's annual battles over taxes (government income) and spending. Nonetheless, whether you are now in a comfortable financial position or overburdened with debt, a disciplined program of saving and spending will give you greater control over your finances. Careful financial planning will tell you where your money is going; you can then plan for a secure future.

The emphasis of any financial program should be its purpose. Your plan should work toward achieving your goals, for example, buying a house. After identifying your goals, give serious consideration to how much they will cost and how you will reach them. You must give yourself an estimate and a deadline; for example, you will need $20,000 in four years to have a down payment for a house. This book provides guidelines and suggestions, but the next, important step is up to you: you must implement the plan you design.

The emphasis of any financial program should be its purpose. Your plan should work toward achieving your goals, for example, buying a house.

The following budget plan may be adapted for two groups of people: those who earn regular salaries or wages (with or without other sources of income) and those whose income is uncertain and irregular. The plan is broken down into three steps: Step I examines income, Step II plots fixed expenses, and Step III controls your variable expenses and allows you to alter your budgeting plans.

While those experienced with budgeting usually plan ahead for a calendar year (the period illustrated), a new budgeter may prefer to set up a shorter program. Start with a three-month trial period. You can expand it later. It is a good idea to pencil in projected figures so you can confirm or change them later. Ink or ballpoint entries are difficult to change.

Step I. The pattern of your income

If you are steadily employed, you can probably forecast your income for the year. You also know what additional sources of income you usually have, such as savings bank interest, dividends, regular gifts, bonuses, income tax refunds, and income from rentals, profitable hobbies, or part-time work.

Draw a chart with 15 columns as indicated below:

Source of Cash Funds	Jan.	Feb.	Mar.	(etc. . . . . . Dec.)								Total	Notes
Take-home pay:													
Husband													
Wife													
Interest													
Dividends													
Other													
Total													

Project your figures across the year (or shorter period). If you expect a raise, change the entries *after* you receive it. A smart policy in money management is never to spend money in advance or even to plan on covering essentials with money you have yet to receive. Many people have trouble with credit payments because the money they counted on failed to come through. A safer strategy is to budget on a minimum basis.

If you are employed, your company does part of your budgeting before you receive your paycheck. Accompanying your check is a breakdown of deductions made for federal, state, and city taxes, Social Security (FICA), state disability insurance, health insurance, and perhaps a pension fund or individual retirement account (IRA). The last four items are assets rather than liabilities, since you have protection and possible financial return from them.

If you are self-employed, you must set aside funds to meet the above commitments yourself. Taxes must be estimated and paid quarterly; you are responsible for Social Security payments; you need health insurance; you should have a personal pension plan, such as a Keogh plan and perhaps an IRA to cover your retirement needs.

Make an estimate for savings bank interest and dividends. You might pencil in last year's figures as a guide. (If you never draw on interest, dividends, or other income for living expenses, but maintain these amounts in your savings and investment program, omit the figures from a budget.) Meeting all financial commitments from take-home pay will help you save for long-term goals such as home ownership, a new car, vacations, and education expenses.

If your employment is irregular, or depends on business profits or commissions, you will probably have to use last year's figures or a reasonable estimate in your projection. The person who receives income in large amounts at irregular intervals may be prone to spending sprees followed by borrowing to meet the inevitable bills. If you are in this category, start now to discipline yourself; be conservative in your spending plans. You may find it helpful to add expected income for the year, divide it by 12, and to allow yourself only one-twelfth for each month's expenses. You are then on the same basis as the regular wage earner, but because your total is uncertain until received, you should exercise restraint in spending.

Finish Step I with a line of monthly totals.

Step II. Programming your commitments

Draw a 15-column form similar to that used in Step I.

Fixed Expenses	(January through December)													Total	Notes
Total															

Under the main heading of Fixed Expenses, note these obligations:

Additional federal, state, and city taxes
Mortgage or rent
Repayments of all loans and installment purchases
Insurance premiums
Telephone, electricity, heating fuel, water, garbage collection, etc.
Pledged contributions
Society or union dues
Savings for future goals and emergencies

You know when these fixed expenses have to be paid. Some are of predictable amounts, such as rent or insurance premiums, and you can project them across 12 months. Some are variable, such as the telephone bill. Use previous bills or estimate this type of payment.

Note that Step II does not include department store and similar billings, only installment payments, if any. This step is designed to cover your fixed expenses of which regular savings should be a part.

Step III. The key to your budget

You now have a total line for your income (Step I), and one for your fixed expenses (Step II). Copy your Step II totals under those of Step I. To arrive at Step III, subtract Step II figures from Step I. The result shows what you have available for your everyday variable expenses.

	(January through December)												Total
Step I													
(total income)													
Step II													
(fixed expenses)													
Available for													
Step III													
(everyday													
expenses)													

No doubt your Step III line is uneven because you have heavier expenses in one month than in another. Perhaps the expenses of some months will be so heavy that you are in the red for your everyday expenditures. Also, some months may show few, if any, fixed expenses.

Here are ways to make an adjustment:

Some people add the heavy obligations that only come up once or twice a year, divide the total by 12, and bank that sum monthly. By so averaging, they prepare for vacations, taxes, insurance premiums, and education expenses.

TOTAL COST

Taxes	$_____
Insurance	_____
Heating	_____
Vacation	_____
Education	_____
Total	$_____

Total ÷ 12 = amount to be set aside monthly

On the other hand, you may want to consider each item separately and project the figures across the budget form.

People with few fixed expenses may prefer to adjust their form simply by raising the savings in Step II so that Step III figures are more or less even each month.

The aim is to arrive at a consistent monthly figure for everyday expenses in line with the budget you draw up in Step III.

As you can see, it will be necessary for you to work backward and forward on these steps before you can develop the best plan to reach your objectives.

Throughout your early budget experiments, remind yourself that you will need at least a full year of record keeping before you can arrive at reasonably settled forms and figures. Often people assume they can solve their financial difficulties overnight by just filling in suggested forms. Usually, a personal financial situation is far too complex for such an easy solution. In the case of a family, it is even more so.

You must record your present expenditures for a time before you can settle on a projected plan for everyday expenses. Only by seeing how much you are spending in certain categories can you set up an improved pattern.

Throughout your early budget experiments, remind yourself that you will need at least a full year of record keeping before you can arrive at reasonably settled forms and figures.

Both married couples and singles will have to set up parts of their budget on a tentative and experimental basis, but keeping track of all spending will provide invaluable records. It is absolutely necessary to good money management to know exactly where your money is going.

Some budgeters, once in the habit of diligent record keeping, prefer to continue it. However, most find it too constricting, and once they have established a suitable amount for a particular category, such as food, stay within that limit. Plan on at least two months of strict record keeping in which all members of the family participate, and note that if you begin in summer, your spending patterns may be different in winter. A seasonal budget readjustment may be required.

Categories of everyday costs

Base daily accounting on the headings you intend to use when making up your budget. Following is a list of suggested main categories and the types for expenditure which would be entered under each:

Food. In this category, include food bought for meals at home, school lunches, and all meals out. Alcoholic beverages, soft drinks, and candy should be included, as well as taxes and tips.

Household maintenance. Repairs, supplies, paid help or services.

Furnishings and equipment. Furniture, floor coverings, accessories such as tableware, curtains, television, radios, etc., and cleaning of any items.

Clothing. Purchase of new clothes, dry cleaning, laundry, and charges by tailor and dressmaker.

Transportation. Automobile payments, upkeep, and operation; commuting expenses; air, train, bus, and taxi fares.

. . . avoid overanalysis. It can prove tiresome and discouraging unless it serves a particular aim.

Health care. Fees for professional medical services, including hospital, drugs, supplies, and eyeglasses.

Education. Textbooks, supplies, tuition. ⟶ or.

Recreation. Entertainment, reading, hobby material, games.

Personal care. Beauty parlor and barber's charges, toiletries, etc.

Family allowances. Each person's spending money.

In general, avoid overanalysis. It can prove tiresome and discouraging unless it serves a particular aim. For example, the cost of dining out can be combined with other food expenses unless you are reporting it as a business expense or you need to determine where the food dollars are going. Of course, you will need a breakdown and receipts of items you deduct for income tax purposes, or need to record for inventory or insurance purposes. Also, you may wish to separate cash from check transactions.

Methods of record keeping

You can note all spending in a small book or pad which can be carried in your purse or pocket. Receipts and store tapes should be kept in a box or drawer at home. Enter all payments on a form drawn up in accordance with your personal or family situation and your need for specific details.

Here is a suggestion:

Date	Food		Clothing		Housing			Transportation		Health		Personal			Etc.
	At home	Out	Pur-chases	Cleaning Repairs	Phone	Supplies	Furnish-ings	Car	Other	Doctor Drugs	Den-tist	Allow-ance, hair care	Drinks tobacco candy		
Total															

Draw up a form best suited to your own everyday expenses. Note that, in the above chart, the telephone bill is under everyday expenses. Earlier, we showed it on Step II as a fixed expense. You can treat it as it best suits you, or split the set rental and usage charges from excess charges, especially if you wish to place a limit on family calls.

Since record keeping is to account for everyday expenses, we omit the Step II (page 16) items, such as rent, insurance, and utilities. Nevertheless, you may want to record them separately so that at the end of a month you can accurately show:

> Total income for month ____
> Less: total expenditure for the month ____
> Cash in hand to meet a saving or
> spending goal ____

Assessing your spending

If you are not overspending, your job is easy. You have only to keep on the same track, perhaps making a few adjustments within certain categories. Even better, if, after subtracting monthly expenses from income, you show a saving, you have money in hand to bank or to satisfy other goals.

Many people find they have overspent, using money that should have been saved; or they have covered expenditures by withdrawing money already saved; or, worse still, they have borrowed to cover expenses. If you have overspent, trim spending for next month. Let your spending goals wait until you have a surplus. Reduce buying on credit to avoid paying additional money for interest. Be patient with your record keeping and planning. You may have to allocate more to clothes, for example, when children need outfitting for school; plans for household purchases may have to be shelved temporarily. Different expenses will come up, but stay within the amount allocated for the flexible expenses for that period.

Your Step III budget form

After you have been keeping records for a time, you can project figures on an annual basis (though you may not find it practical to plan closely for more than two or three months in advance). A form is suggested below.

	Jan.	Feb.	Mar.	Apr.	May	Jun.	Jul.	Aug.	Sep.	Oct.	Nov.	Dec.	Notes
Food													
Housing													
Clothes													
etc.													
etc.													
Total													

If you set up a record of what you actually spent and compare it with your plan, you will have a useful guide to help you to cut back—and to maintain a vital reserve fund.

At times, of course, your control over Step III expenditures may break down. Unexpected medical bills may roll in at the same time you have to pay the plumber, painter, and roofer, or the rent goes up when you can least afford the extra payment. The only sound answer to such emergencies is to have a reserve in your savings account. Financial advisors suggest you keep at least three months' income as a reserve fund.

Until you have that reserve, set a minimum figure for your everyday expenditures, and make the necessary adjustments within that figure. Cut down on spending that is not essential so that the reserve can be increased.

Upcoming variable bills

An expense which frequently breaks the new budget is the charge account. Weeks after a purchase is made, the bill arrives. If provision has not been made for its payment and you cannot pay on time, extra interest charges will be incurred on the account.

An expense which frequently breaks the new budget is the charge account.

You should keep a record of credit spending so that you will be ready for the billing. Note the billing date of each department store or bank credit card you have; if one company bills on the 6th of the month and another on the 16th and you are paid twice a month, you can set aside some money from each paycheck to cover payments.

If you are using your budget, you should generally not buy in excess of planned items. But because people do sometimes buy on impulse, a record of charges will help in adjusting next month's plan to meet the expected bills.

Use savings accounts in budget plans

Passbook savings accounts at local banks and thrift institutions are valuable tools for budgeting. You can set aside funds in an account until needed to pay bills.

Your regular savings. Savings have been listed in your budget plan as a definite commitment to be handled as regularly and seriously as paying taxes. Savings objectives might include an emergency fund, vacation, gifts, down payment on a house, investments, education costs, retirement, home improvements, furniture, major appliances. Some are long-term, some short-term goals.

Using credit on a budget

Being on a budget does not mean paying only in cash and not using credit cards. Establishing a sound credit record is important in today's society, so a budget allows for the use of credit cards when necessary. However, limit credit spending to the amount you could pay in cash. Let your money accumulate interest in a savings account until payment on bills is due.

Budgeting for investments

Investments in stocks, mutual funds, and Treasury notes and bills are discussed in later chapters. But the first step for many individuals and families will be the accumulation of savings which can eventually be channeled into high-return, possibly tax-exempt, investments for which minimum initial payments

---

Establishing a sound credit record is important in today's society, so a budget allows for the use of credit cards when necessary. However, limit credit spending to the amount you could pay in cash.

---

are necessary. While savings in banks and thrift institutions are insured, the same is not true for many other forms of investment. Therefore, before venturing into possible areas of risk or tying up your funds, establish a substantial cushion for emergencies and for fluctuating family needs.

Establishing your net worth

No financial program for the future can be made without determining where you stand today, and annually thereafter.

The forms given below will help you make your tabulations. Add and delete headings to suit your situation, but make sure you cover all items that add to your total worth and every liability against it.

To complete your statement, you may need to ask your insurance agent, your employer, and your bank for figures on annuities, retirement funds, and U.S. Savings Bonds.

Be objective when you value property such as your home, automobile, household equipment, and personal items. What

Annual Financial Statement   (Date)

Assets

Cash on hand	$_____
Checking accounts	_____
Savings accounts	_____
Money lent to others (repayment expected)	_____
Value of life insurance (cash surrender value plus dividend accumulations)	_____
Annuities	_____
Retirement funds	_____
U.S. Savings Bonds	_____
Investments—	
Stocks, bonds, mutual fund shares	_____
Real estate	_____
Pension and profit-sharing plans	_____
Your home—full market value	_____
Other property—current value (list such items as)	
Automobile	_____
Household furnishings	_____
Furs, jewelry	_____
Sports and hobby items	_____
Total Assets	$_____

Liabilities

Unpaid Bills

    Charge accounts $_____

    Credit card accounts   _____

    Taxes   _____

    Insurance premiums   _____

    Other   _____

Balances Due on—

    Installment contracts   _____

    Loans (from banks, savings and loan

        associations, insurance companies,

        etc.)   _____

    Other   _____

Mortgages payable on home and other

    property (or rent)   _____

                Total Liabilities $_____

Summary

Assets $_____

Liabilities   − _____

                Net Worth $_____

would they bring in today's market? For example, have your neighborhood property values appreciated or depreciated? The real estate section of your local newspaper is a useful source of information for property prices. The *Kelley Blue Book* will help you make a realistic estimate of your car's worth. Personal property is hard to value. Sports equipment may depreciate, but antiques, paintings, and hobby collections could appreciate in value. Newspaper advertisements and the columns of specialty journals at the library may help you make an assessment of your property's worth.

Use today's quotations to value stocks, bonds, mutual shares. Disregard any gains or losses that may occur later.

With your net worth established, you and your family can plan for the year. You are in a position to make a five-year plan, as business and governments do, and can gear income and expenses to the fulfillment of your objectives. Note, too, that net worth data are essential to planning for retirement and for your estate.

Your family records

To calculate your net worth, you have to refer to many personal papers. Family records will, of course, differ according to the assets owned, but the location of all records should be set down. If a loose-leaf notebook is used, it is easy to make photocopies of the pages. Duplicate family records can be given to adult children or kept at your office. Printed record books are available, but you may prefer to make your own in line with your other financial records and inventories of valuables.

Here are some important items which should be listed with a note of reference about their location: certificates of birth, marriage, divorce, death, naturalization, and adoption papers. Such official documents are essential to prove date and place of birth, to obtain American citizenship for the foreign-born, to obtain a passport, to collect on insurance, to remarry, to claim Social Security benefits, etc. If any of these certificates is missing, obtain a certified copy. A certified copy of a birth or death certificate can be obtained at your state or city's central vital statistics office, usually associated with the Department of Health.

Social Security. Members of your family who have Social Security cards should make a note of the numbers and where the cards are usually kept. The cards come in two parts; keep one stub with other important records. Then, if a card is lost, the stub can be mailed to your local Social Security office with a request for a duplicate. You must supply name, address, and place of business, in addition to the number.

Bank accounts. List bank names and addresses with the numbers of savings and checking accounts and the names of the family members who own each one. Each year, banks advertise for missing depositors who have either forgotten their accounts or died without informing their relatives of them. See that the necessary information is available in your family.

United States Savings Bonds. Maintain a careful record of your bonds, noting full serial numbers, issue dates, and denomination. If the bonds are lost, stolen, or destroyed, send such information at once to the Bureau of the Public Department, Division of Loans and Currency, 536 South Clark Street, Chicago, Illinois 60605. You will receive full information on how to get replacements.

Insurance of all types. Record information about each policy, its number, amount payable, and method of settlement. Include information about personal coverage at your place of business, such as participation in group health, pension, or profit-sharing plans. List names and addresses of all companies involved and state where the policies are kept.

Credit cards. Legislation and other protective measures taken by issuers of credit cards have reduced the responsibility of cardholders for fraudulent use of their cards. Nevertheless, you should list all your account numbers and the name and address of each issuing company. Advise loss of your card immediately by phone or wire, and confirm in writing.

Your safe deposit box

For a small sum, a safe deposit box can be rented at your bank or thrift institution. Here you can safeguard valuable jewelry, stock certificates, deeds, legal records of all types, passports, bankbooks, personal papers, and your household inventory. Your will is best left with your attorney, but a copy should go in the box.

Guard the keys to the box because you are the sole possessor. The bank does not keep a duplicate. You should appoint a deputy who can open the box in case you cannot. Check with the bank on its regulations affecting deputies.

Also, discuss with your attorney the legal implications which might arise, particularly at time of death, if you rent the safe deposit box jointly with your spouse.

The contents of a safe deposit box are usually insured only against theft by a bank employee. Read the agreement you sign when you rent the box. Under most agreements, the bank is not liable in case of fire or other natural disaster. If there is a robbery, the bank may be liable only if negligence can be proven. For your protection, keep in a safe place at home photocopies of all important papers stored in the box. You may also buy insurance on the contents of your safe deposit box; a common method is to add a rider to your homeowner's policy.

Chapter 2

INVESTING FOR INTEREST INCOME

INFLATION and increased short-term government borrowing have revolutionized the way Americans save. Where safety was once a predominant concern, high returns have become the current chief objective. The change in savings patterns was marked by the widespread switch from bank account savings to investments in high-yielding money market funds, Treasury bills, and short-term bank certificates. In addition, these investments provided an opportunity to earn high income and park cash during periods of uncertainty in the stock and other investment markets.

As a result of this switch, savings institutions have lost their monopoly on the savings of individuals. However, they are now learning to compete by providing not only convenient local services but also by offering returns comparable to market rates.

To reflect the current options in interest investments, this chapter is divided into three parts: (1) investments in money market funds, Treasury obligations, and bonds; (2) savings in financial institutions; and (3) a discussion of how to determine which investment suits your income and financial requirements.

29

Part I. THE MONEY MARKET
Money market funds

The popularity of money market funds is traceable to the spectacular rise in interest rates. When interest rates were at record highs, money funds fared extremely well; in 1981 assets jumped from approximately $75 billion to more than $180 billion. Investors turned to money market funds for high yields; they had an average pre-tax return of 16.8% in 1981.

Even in periods of declining interest rates, money market funds have continued to hold investors. The reason: They provide a handy parking place for cash which can be easily switched to the stock market or other investment. Most money market funds allow deposits to be withdrawn at any time without penalty.

Money market funds pool the cash of many investors to lend to large institutions. These loans are short term, for periods ranging from overnight to a few months. Investments are made in Treasury bills and other securities issued by the United States government and its agencies, bank certificates of deposit, high-grade commercial paper, letters of credit, and other short-term debt securities. Some funds concentrate heavily on one type of instrument, such as government securities. Yields change daily and are not guaranteed.

Even in periods of declining interest rates, money market funds have continued to hold investors. The reason: They provide a handy parking place for cash which can be easily switched to the stock market or other investment.

Money market funds are not federally insured, but are considered relatively safe investments by most experts. Some state-chartered banks have begun offering money market funds insured by a state insurance fund. The majority of funds invest in securities with maturities no greater than 30 to 60 days, and many funds keep 25% or more of their assets in overnight instruments. Funds have been careful to maintain short-term maturities to assure the availability of cash in case of an unexpected surge in redemption requests. Even in the face of massive redemptions, a fund should be able to sell enough short-term securities to meet the demand within a week or two. Without short-term holdings, a fund might have to sell off assets at a loss, thereby reducing the value of its shares below their regular $1 per share value; redeeming investors would lose money. Most experts believe this danger is reduced by a fund's short-term portfolio.

Nevertheless, since the funds are uninsured, an investor must use caution. Research a fund before investing. There are investment services which publish safety ratings for different funds from the highest, rated AAA, to AA, BBB, B, C, and D. Your broker may have this information. The highest ratings generally go to funds with the shortest average portfolio maturities and the greatest diversification of holdings. As important as safety is, an investor need not worry about the differences between AAA and AA funds. The difference in risk is minimal, so an AA fund with a higher yield may be preferable to a lower yielding AAA fund.

For the cautious investor, there are money funds which invest only in government securities. All of these are rated AAA. For the extra security, the investor accepts a reduced yield, usually about 1% less than other AAA or AA funds.

Money market funds advertise widely. By calling a toll-free number or using a mail-in coupon from an advertisement appearing in the financial pages of newspapers and business journals, you can receive a prospectus listing portfolio information, charges, and expenses, and telling you how you can invest.

Money market funds differ on minimum initial investments; $1,000, $2,500, or $5,000 is often required. The funds are listed in financial publications among other mutual funds, under the "family" heading when they are one of a few types of funds managed by one company. The Net Asset Value (NAV) is stated as $1 and often followed by N.L. for "no-load," which means no finance or sales charge. But a fund might have a monthly maintenance charge which would weigh more heavily against a small account than a large one.

Gains and losses are generally not realized in money market funds. Shares are redeemed for exactly what you paid (usually $1 per share) plus accrued interest. Most money market funds allow you to write checks for $500 or more on your fund account. Your money continues to earn interest until the check clears, which may be days later. Withdrawals may be requested by mail, wire, or telephone.

Treasury obligations

Treasury bills, bonds, and notes have attracted investors for two reasons: (1) interest is not taxed at the state and local level; (2) the investment is secure, backed by the full faith and credit of the United States government. At times of high interest rates, a third factor operates: short-term Treasuries offer a competitive return.

Treasury bills are direct obligations of the Treasury, issued to finance budgetary needs. Maturities run for 3 months, 6 months, and 12 months on bills, two to ten years on notes, and more than ten years on bonds. Bills are available in denominations of $10,000, $15,000, $50,000, $100,000, and $1 million; some bonds and notes require only a $1,000 minimum investment.

Buying Treasury bills. The bills are sold at a discount at Treasury auctions held at the Federal Reserve Banks, which serve as agents for the Treasury. They are redeemed at face value, so your return is the difference between the discount price you pay for the bill and its face value if you hold it to maturity, or the amount you receive if you sell it before maturity.

You may buy Treasury bills directly, without charge, from any Federal Reserve Bank, which gives you a receipt indicating that a book entry of your purchase has been recorded. You may also buy or sell Treasury bills through your bank or broker who will charge you for the transaction. Treasury bills are usually auctioned each Monday, or on the previous Friday when Monday is a holiday.

Figuring the yield on your Treasury bill. The difference between the average price and the face value of the Treasury bill is the discount at which the bill is sold. Your tender is filled at this price and, if you buy your bill direct, a check for this difference is mailed to you on the issue date of the bills. If you buy through a bank, the bank will credit your account with the discount. For example, assume that the accepted average bid on three-month bills is $9,700. You give the government $10,000. To reflect the actual purchase price of $9,700, a "discount" check of $300 is mailed to you. The discount is interest income taxable in the year the bill matures; at maturity, you of course receive $10,000.

The equivalent annual yield on your bill is figured this way:

1. Find the yield on your investment by dividing the discount by the purchase price.
2. Convert this yield to the annual rate by dividing the yield by .2500 if the bill is a three-month one, by .5000 for a six-month bill.

On a three-month bill if your discount is $300 (cost: $9,700), the equivalent annual yield is .1236, or 12.36%.

$$\frac{\$300}{\$9,700} = .0309; \frac{.0309}{.2500} = .1236 \text{ or } 12.36\% \text{ per year}$$

Financial pages of daily newspapers report the previous day's auction, including the discount rate and what this amounts to as an annual percentage yield.

Cashing bills before maturity. If you need funds before the maturity date of your bill, you can sell it through a commercial bank or a securities broker. The Federal Reserve Bank and the Treasury do not handle bills which have not matured.

For bills sold before maturity, current interest rates determine the amount you will receive.

After maturity. Unless you notify the Federal Reserve Bank that you wish to roll over matured bills into new bills, redemption is automatic at maturity. The Treasury will mail you a check for the amount of your bill. If you bought your bill through a bank, the bank will credit your account on the date the bill matures. If you wish to roll over your maturing bill, you follow the same procedures as in buying a new bill, using your matured bill as payment. A discount check for the difference between the price of the new bill and the face value of your matured bill will be mailed to you on the issue date of the new bill.

Buying Treasury notes and bonds. These securities are not sold on a regular schedule. Contact the nearest Federal Reserve Bank or branch for information and notification of sales. Financial publications also give notice of upcoming sales.

The payment of interest on notes and bonds is not the same as for bills. While Treasury bills are discounted so that buyers receive an immediate return shortly after purchase, interest on notes and bonds is paid semiannually.

Taxation of Treasury obligations. Although interest escapes tax at the state and local level, it is subject to federal income tax. However, the discount on three- and six-month T-bills is not taxed until the bill matures even though it is received shortly after the purchase. For bills bought later in the year, it means the deferral of income tax to the following year. For example, you buy a six-month T-bill in August 1982 at $9,400. You receive a check for $600 shortly thereafter. Since the bill matures in February 1983, the $600 is not taxed until 1983.

Obligations of U.S. agencies

In addition to Treasury obligations, an investor can turn to the obligations of various federal agencies. Some of these obligations carry full faith and credit of the United States, some have only an implied guarantee, and some no backing from the federal government, but risk is generally considered negligible. Because investors are less acquainted with these issues than with Treasury obligations, they do not sell as readily on the secondary market.

Some but not all agency obligations escape income tax on state and local levels.

Purchases of agency obligations are made through commercial banks or brokers at a similar charge as Treasury issue purchases. (Where the charge is the same for large, long-term transactions as for small, short-term purchases, the investor must consider the effect on overall yield.) U.S. agency securities generally have minimums of $5,000, $10,000, or $25,000, but some may be available for as little as $1,000. Units of certificates (for example, Government National Mortgage Association [GNMA] pass-throughs) can be bought for $1,000. Inquire about the different types of obligations issued by Banks for Cooperatives, Federal Home Loan Bank, Federal Land Banks, as well as GNMA and FNMA (Federal National Mortgage Association), and other agencies. You might also consider mutual funds that invest in the obligations of government agencies.

Corporate bonds

When you buy a corporate bond, you are lending money to the issuer of the bonds. You become a creditor of the issuing company; you are not a part owner as is a stockholder. The corporation pledges to pay you interest on specified dates, generally twice a year, and to repay the principal on the date of maturity stated on the bond.

For investment purposes, a bond may be described according to the length of its period of maturity. Short-term bonds usually mature within 1 to 5 years; medium-term bonds in 5 to 20 years; long-term bonds in 20 or more years.

Where the interest is paid out on a regular schedule, the bond is called a current income bond. An accrual or discount bond is a bond on which interest is accumulated and paid as part of the specified maturity value (the bond having been issued at a price lower than the specified maturity value).

Interest on bearer bonds issued with coupons attached is paid when a bondholder clips the coupon and deposits it for payment. A registered bond carries the name of the owner, who receives his interest by mail from the issuing corporation.

Whether a bond is registered or in bearer form has no effect on its investment quality or yield. A coupon-type or bearer bond may be preferred by institutional investors because it can be transferred by hand without registration. However, this advantage must be weighed against the risks of loss through fire, theft, or casualty.

Issuing and trading of bonds. New bond issues are generally placed through investment bankers who usually assist in the preparation of the issue. Often an issue may be sold directly by the issuing organization to an institutional investor. Many newly issued bonds are purchased directly from issuers or from their investment bankers by institutional investors each year before the bonds are offered to individual investors. Issuers prefer this type of placement since it involves less expense than a public offering. Normally, only the new issues (or part of new issues) which cannot be marketed this way are offered to private investors.

Bonds are also traded on the open market where individuals, as well as institutional buyers, may buy or sell them at competitive, market-determined prices, through dealers or brokers. Bondholders buy and sell bonds as interest rates change.

Investment return on a bond is generally limited to the stated interest. You cannot expect any appreciation of principal as you can in a stock investment, unless you have bought bonds selling at a discount.

Daily bond sales and prices on the major exchanges are listed in the prominent financial dailies. Bond prices fluctuate in response to the changes in interest rates and business conditions. In setting the daily price of a bond, the market weighs the current status, performance, and future prospects of the issuing corporation, as well as the interest rate and maturity period of the bond. Quotations are based on 100 as equal to par, even though the basic unit for an actual bond may be in denominations of $1,000. A quote of 90½ simply means a bond with a face value of $1,000 will cost $905 at market.

Figuring the yield on a bond. The investment value of bonds is generally expressed in rates of yield. There are four types of yield: the nominal or coupon yield; the actual yield; the current market yield; and the net yield to maturity. The nominal or coupon yield is the fixed or contractual rate of interest stated on the bond. A bond paying 11% has a nominal yield of 11%. The actual yield is the rate of return based on the price at which the bond was purchased. If bought below par, the actual yield will exceed the nominal or coupon yield. If bought at a premium (above par) the actual yield will be less than the coupon or nominal yield. For example, if you paid $800 for a $1,000 bond paying 10% interest, the actual yield is 12½% ($100 divided by $800).

The current market yield is the rate of return on the bond if bought at prevailing market price. It is figured in the same manner as actual yield. (However, current market yield will fluctuate daily.) For example, if the 10% bond is quoted at $750, its current yield on that day would be 13⅓%.

Net yield to maturity represents the rate of return on the bond if it is held to maturity, plus appreciation allocated to a discount purchase or less reductions for any premium paid on a bond selling above par. If you buy a bond below par at a market discount, your annual return is proportionately increased by a part of the discount allocated to the number of years before maturity. If the discount was $50 on a bond having a five-year maturity, your annual income return on the bond is increased by $10 ($50 divided by 5). On the other hand, if you bought at a premium, the extra cost is a reduction against your income because you paid more than can be recovered at maturity. This cost is allocated over the remaining life of the bond. Thus if you bought a five-year bond at $50 over par, your average annual return is reduced by $10 ($50 divided by 5).

Call privileges may reduce the investment value of the bond. A call privilege gives the issuer a chance to redeem the obligation before maturity if interest rates have declined below the rate fixed by the obligation. The existence of a call is a disadvantage to an investor; it may deprive him of a favorable investment at a time he may not be able to replace it with another. To take some of the sting out of a call provision, the issuer may provide for the payment of a "premium" on the exercise of the call and a minimum period during which the bonds will not be called.

The amount of the premium varies with the length of period in which the bond may be called. As the maturity date approaches, the call premium will decrease. Some bonds now carry a guarantee that they will not be called for a specified number of years, often five or ten years.

A call privilege will generally not be exercised if the going interest rate remains about the same as, or is higher than, the interest rate of the bond. If interest rates decline below the interest rate of the bond, the bond will probably be called because the issuer can obtain the borrowed money at lower cost elsewhere.

Calls under sinking fund redemption. A bond may be called in at par under the terms of a sinking fund, which the company sets aside as a reserve for eventual redemption of the bonds. Not all bonds are called and those that are selected are picked by lot. Redemptions for sinking fund purposes account for only a small percentage of a single bond issue. But some issues may retain the right to use a blanket sinking fund under which they may redeem bonds paying interest at their highest rate.

Put privileges. A put privilege is the flip side of a call privilege. It permits the buyer to sell the bonds at par to the issuer after a stated number of years. This feature is valuable to investors for long-term bonds. If interest rates rise, investors are not locked into low yields.

How interest rates affect the selling price of bonds

If current interest rates increase over the interest rate of your bond, the market value of your bond will decline. The decline in value has nothing to do with the credit rating of the issue. It simply means that other investors will buy only at terms that will give them the current higher return. If you bought a bond paying a rate of 8% at face value (par), $1,000, and a few months later interest rates go to 11%, another investor will not pay $1,000 for a bond with an 8% return. To match the 11% return, the market value of the

---

Thus during periods of rising interest rates, the price of bonds issued at lower rates in prior years declines. This occurs even to top-quality bonds; the highest credit rating will not protect the market value of a low-interest-paying bond.

---

bond will drop to a level which will return 11% on the money invested, based on its actual 8% return and the period remaining before maturity. Thus during periods of rising interest rates, the price of bonds issued at lower rates in prior years declines. This occurs even to top-quality bonds; the highest credit rating will not protect the market value of a low-interest-paying bond. When this happens there may be bond bargains available, as prices on outstanding bonds decrease. Bonds bought at deep discounts will yield capital gains if held to maturity. The difference between what you paid and the par value received at maturity is a long-term capital gain subject to favorable tax rates. For example, if you buy a $10,000 14-year 7% bond selling at 62.12, you pay only $6,212. If held to maturity you will receive $10,000, giving you a $3,788 long-term capital gain ($10,000 less $6,212 cost). If you are in the 40% bracket, your profit after capital gains taxes is $3,182; if in the 50% bracket, your after-tax profit is $3,030.

If interest rates decline below the interest rate of your bond, the value of your bond will increase, but at the same time the issuing company, if it has an exercisable call option, may redeem the bond to rid itself of the high interest cost and attempt to raise funds at current lower rates. Thus an early redemption of the bond could upset your long-range investment plans in that particular issue.

A zero coupon bond allows an investor to lock in a return. He knows how much he will have at maturity and so avoids the problem of turning over his investments at fluctuating short-term rates.

With these points in mind, you can understand why in recent years investors shied away from long-term bonds when volatile interest rates ran into double digits. Investors preferred the high short-term rates. The effect of the investor flight from long-term issues hurt the ability of lenders to raise funds and forced them to devise new types of issues, such as zero coupon bonds and floating-rate bonds.

Zero coupon bonds. A zero coupon bond is a deep-discount obligation which has come into fashion among companies which have found it difficult to market traditional long-term bonds. The zero coupon bond allows them to compete during periods of high interest rates. The bonds are issued at considerably less than face value and redeemed at face at a set date. No annual interest is paid. A zero coupon bond allows an investor to lock in a return. He knows how much he will have at maturity and so avoids the problem of turning over his investments at fluctuating short-term rates. For example, one zero coupon bond sold at 33.24% of par. This meant a $1,000 face bond could be bought for $332.40 and return $1,000 when the bond matures in eight years, giving an effective yield of 14.25%. However, a zero coupon bond may not be an attractive investment because of this tax consequence: interest is reported annually, even though, in fact, none is received. There are some cases where this tax cost is not an impediment so that a zero coupon bond is worth considering, such as in an individual retirement account investment, since IRA income is not taxed until distributions from the IRA are made. Whether zero coupon bonds are a better choice for an IRA than other investments depends on prevailing interest rates and an "informed" guess at the future. If an investor expects interest rates to drop significantly from current rates, a zero coupon bond has the advantage of guaranteeing current yield.

Zero coupon bonds may also be a means of financing a child's education. A parent buys the bond for the child. The child must report the income, but as the child is probably in a low tax bracket, little or no tax may be due.

Floating-rate or variable-interest bonds. For investors unwilling to gamble on the future of interest rates, some bonds now offer floating interest rates. The rate is updated periodically, but there may be a floor and ceiling limiting the changes. The market price of the bond should remain near par since its interest rate moves with the market. Although this feature is a form of insurance for the investor, it may not be worth its added cost.

To have the benefit of the floating rate, a buyer receives a lower yield. If interest rates fall in the future, the buyer's return decreases, and the buyer will not be able to take advantage of the dropping interest rate. Thus he cannot earn capital gains.

The timing of the interest adjustments also affects these bonds. An adjustment every six months is too infrequent to

keep up with market changes. Some issues of floating-rate
bonds now update the interest payment every month. The
method used to calculate the interest changes will also affect
the yield.

Unit investment trusts

Investment houses offer unit investment trusts which hold
portfolios of securities. Yield is fixed for the life of the trust
with interest payable semiannually or more frequently. As
securities in the portfolio mature, a unit holder receives a repayment of principal. Unit trusts provide investors with the
possibility of locking into current yields for the long term. However, a trust has this disadvantage: if principal is needed
before the end of the trust term, an investor may sacrifice substantial amounts of principal if interest rates rise or if the general investment market is shying away from long-term investments; even where the trust may offer a current return equal
to market value, its price may be depressed because there may
be few investors willing to take the risk of tying up their funds
in long-term investments. Despite these drawbacks, the performance of unit trusts has been rated higher than that of
similar mutual funds.

Unit trusts hold varying types of debt instruments. Municipal bond trusts, made up of tax-exempt obligations, are generally favored by investors in the top tax brackets. Taxable
unit trusts hold investments such as corporate bonds, bank
certificates of deposit, and Treasury obligations. Floating-rate
tax-exempt unit trusts are available soon, offering features that
maintain principal without sacrificing the certainty of return
common to unit trusts. Still, the investor looking for high
quality can continue to find unit trusts made up of A, AA,
and AAA securities. Usually, units are offered in denominations of $1,000. An investor pays a front-end sales charge but
no management fee as there is no need for management once
a unit trust is closed.

Maturities of the various trusts range as follows: the short-
term, tax-exempt average is 3 years; intermediate, 6 to 12
years; and long term, 18 to 30 years. An average for corporate intermediate is 6 years, 25 for long term.

Investing in tax-exempts

Tax-exempt obligations are issued by state and local governments. Their attraction: Interest is not subject to federal income tax or tax of the state in which the obligations are is-

---

To determine if a tax-exempt is a good investment for you, compare the interest return with that of a taxable bond.

---

sued. Despite this break, tax-exempts may not appeal to you because they pay less interest than comparable taxable obligations. To determine if a tax-exempt is a good investment for you, compare the interest return with that of a taxable bond. You figure the taxable return that is equivalent to the tax-free yield of the tax-exempt. This amount depends on your tax bracket. For example, a municipal bond of $5,000 yielding 8% is the equivalent of a taxable yield of 16% if you are in the 50% bracket. The table below shows what a taxable bond would have to earn to equal the tax-exempt bond according to your income tax bracket.

If top income tax rate is—	A tax-exempt yield of*										
	5%	6%	6½%	7%	7½%	8%	8½%	9%	10%	11%	12%
	is the equivalent of these taxable yields:										
19	6.2	7.4	8.0	8.6	9.3	9.9	10.5	11.1	12.3	13.6	14.8
22	6.4	7.7	8.3	9.0	9.6	10.3	10.9	11.5	12.8	14.1	15.4
24	6.6	7.9	8.6	9.2	9.9	10.5	11.2	11.8	13.2	14.5	15.8
28	6.9	8.3	9.0	9.7	10.4	11.1	11.8	12.5	13.9	15.3	16.7
32	7.4	8.8	9.6	10.3	11.0	11.8	12.5	13.2	14.7	16.2	17.6
39	8.2	9.8	10.7	11.5	12.3	13.1	13.9	14.8	16.4	18.0	19.7
42	8.6	10.3	11.2	12.1	12.9	13.8	14.7	15.5	17.2	19.0	20.7
44	8.9	10.7	11.6	12.5	13.4	14.3	15.2	16.1	17.9	19.6	21.4
49	9.8	11.8	12.7	13.7	14.7	15.7	16.7	17.6	19.6	21.6	23.5
50	10.0	12.0	13.0	14.0	15.0	16.0	17.0	18.0	20.0	22.0	24.0

* Exemption from the tax of the state issuing the bond will increase the yield.

If you are considering the purchase of tax-exempts at a discount, make sure you understand the quoted yield. Otherwise, you may find that part of your investment is taxable. A quoted yield includes both interest (which is tax exempt) and potential profit on discount (which will be taxed when and if realized).

Ratings of tax-exempt bonds. Tax-exempt issues are rated by services, such as Standard & Poor's and Moody's. In rating a bond, the services consider the size of the issuer, the amount of its outstanding debt, its record in paying off prior debts, whether it has competent officials and a balanced budget, its tax assessment and collection record, and whether the community is dominated by a single industry which might be subject to economic change. Generally, an issuer with a good credit rating will offer lower interest rates than one plagued with revenue deficits or similar problems. A basic test is the sufficiency of tax yields or revenues even under times of economic stress. General obligation bonds will normally be rated higher than revenue bonds because they have the support of the taxing power of the community. Revenue bonds (backed by the revenue of the issuer, such as bridge tolls on a transportation department bond) may receive high ratings once a capacity to produce earnings is shown.

The market for tax-exempts is not as large as the market for stock. This poses a risk if you ever need ready cash and are forced to sell a tax-exempt bond. You may not be able to find an immediate buyer and may have to sell at a discount. If you are concerned with liquidity, restrict your investments to major general obligation bonds of state governments and revenue bonds of major authorities.

Instead of purchasing tax-exempts directly, consider investing in municipal bond funds.

Tax-exempt municipal bond funds. These funds are open-ended mutual funds which invest in municipal bonds of varied ratings. The prospective investor should examine a fund's portfolio described in its prospectus. One fund may be fully invested in bonds rated A or better, while another may have a more speculative portfolio, say, bonds rated below BBB. A fund with substantial assets in the riskier bonds will offer higher yields in compensation. A fund does not remain static; the function of management is to move with market conditions; moreover, redemptions must be financed. While the aim is to keep both asset value and yield high, even the best management may miss under pressure of unfavorable conditions. As with other bond investments, the resale value of fund shares will decline if interest rates increase. Generally speaking, municipals have, over the years, been considered low-risk investments. But the potential investor must consider economic conditions and trends as well as other factors which might affect a municipality's ability to meet its obligations.

Most tax-exempt bond funds offer the same flexibility possible in other types of mutual funds. You may receive your dividends regularly or have them reinvested for tax-free compounding. You may have a systematic payout plan, if you wish, which is particularly useful at retirement. If you are in a "family" of a few funds managed by one company, you may switch to another type of fund for a low transfer fee. Some funds offer special features, such as free check writing (generally, $500 minimum) and the privilege of redeeming shares by phone or wire.

Generally speaking, municipals have, over the years, been considered low-risk investments. But the potential investor must consider economic conditions and trends as well as other factors which might affect a municipality's ability to meet its obligations.

Redemptions are at net asset value, which may be more or less than value at the time of share purchase.

When you invest directly in a no-load tax-exempt municipal bond fund, there are no sales charges as there are for load funds, which are obtainable from brokers. Management fees are charged by all the funds; many are below 1%. Minimum investments vary: $1,000, $2,500, $5,000 are common.

If you are interested in tax-exempt municipal bond funds, you should also investigate current offerings in unit investment trusts, discussed on page 41.

Tax-exempt notes. Although generally bought by banks and large corporations, short-term tax-exempt notes may sometimes be available to individuals. The majority of notes are offered in face amounts of $25,000 and up, but sometimes in denominations of $5,000 and $10,000. They are issued by states and municipalities to tide them over until expected revenues are received or until longer term money can be raised through an issue of long-term bonds. Where rising interest rates have made the cost of long-term issues high, a government authority may postpone a long-term offering and try to fill the gap with short-term notes. The interest rates on tax-exempt notes are generally higher than on tax-exempt bonds; the authority is generally willing to pay the extra interest for the short term, in the expectation that a future long-term offering may be placed at lower rates.

Interest on these short-term notes is exempt from federal tax. Many of the notes are from housing authorities and issued to pay construction costs on projects for which bonds will eventually be issued. Housing notes are guaranteed by the FHA and, because of their great safety, are not expected to have yields as high as some of the other, more speculative paper.

Part II. SAVING INSTITUTIONS

Types of savings accounts

Commercial banks and thrift institutions (savings banks and savings and loan associations) offer two basic types of savings accounts, passbook and term. However, to attract cus-

---

Passbook accounts make little sense as instruments of saving in inflationary times.

---

tomers, savings institutions are developing high-yield short-term instruments, such as repurchase agreements and money fund accounts. Check banks and thrifts in your area since investments will vary from state to state.

Passbook accounts, held to a maximum interest rate of 5.5% at thrifts and 5.25% at banks, make little sense as instruments of saving in inflationary times. Nevertheless, you may still find them handy for ready access to funds. Most savings institutions offer day-of-deposit to day-of-withdrawal accounts on which you do not lose interest when you make mid-period withdrawals. This type of account has largely replaced the regular savings account on which interest is lost if funds are withdrawn before the end of a quarterly or half-yearly posting period. Many thrift institutions now compound interest daily, and some post interest monthly rather than quarterly, allowing the customer more flexibility. Nevertheless, if you are a saver who can afford to tie up funds for a period, you should transfer as much cash as possible to term accounts earning higher rates.

Note that some savings institutions do not pay interest on balances below a set minimum, such as $50 or $100. The minimum may change without notice. Some savings institutions charge a service fee if a savings account falls below a certain minimum.

Term (or time) accounts require you to keep your savings in the account for a stated period. Savings certificates are the most popular form of term account. All savings institutions do not offer the same types of accounts; investigate the investment options in your area.

Banks are now free to set their own maximum interest rates on certificates of deposit (CDs) with maturities of 32 days or more. These rates are no longer set by law. Rates on bank CDs will follow going rates for money market funds and Treasury bills and notes. Competition between banks gives you the opportunity to shop around for the highest obtainable rate.

Minimum deposits if any also set by the banks. Government regulations no longer require any fixed minimum deposit. Some banks may require an initial deposit depending on the terms of the CD. For example, some banks may require a $2,500 minimum for an account maturing in less than a year and $1,000 on an account maturing in one year or more; other banks may require more or less than these amounts depending on competition in the locality.

A bank may also allow you to choose a specific maturity term for your CD. For example, if in 380 days you will need funds for a specific purpose, such as to pay for a wedding or tuition, you may be allowed to choose a CD with a maturity of 379 days.

The maximum available term for a CD varies from bank to bank. Most banks issue CDs with terms up to five years; some banks may even offer longer terms.

Premature withdrawal penalty

Government regulations impose a penalty for withdrawing principal from time accounts before maturity. For accounts opened on or after October 1, 1983, the penalty is three months' interest if the account's maturity is more than one year. The penalty is one month's interest for accounts with maturities of one year or less.

The penalty is not limited to the amount of interest earned; you could lose some of your principal. For example, on a $10,000 30-month account yielding 10%, the penalty is three months' interest, or $250. If it is closed after two months, $250 will be deducted, even though the account has only earned $166.66. The difference, $83.34, will be deducted from the $10,000 principal.

Larger penalties apply to term accounts opened before October 1, 1983.

The above penalties are the minimum; a bank may establish higher penalties. Banks are required to inform you of penalties when you open a term account. You may deduct the penalty on your income tax return.

If premiums are given for new or increased accounts, funds deposited in return for a gift must remain for a specified period, such as 12 or 14 months. A penalty may be enacted for early withdrawal.

Repurchase agreements (repos)

Some banks offer high-yielding repurchase agreements for a limited period of time to attract funds. They allow you to earn high interest rates by sharing in a portion of the bank's portfolio of government securities. The minimum investment may be as low as $1,000; maturities vary, but the average is about three months. The interest rate you receive at purchase is in effect for the term of the repo, even if interest rates change in the meantime. Repos may be automatically renewed; check in advance.

The disadvantage of repos is that they are not FDIC or FSLIC insured. However, they offer more liquidity than term deposits since the institution is required to repurchase your investment at your request. There is no interest penalty for early repurchase as long as you hold the repo for a minimum period of a week or more. There may be a small service charge for early repurchase.

Banks' insured money market funds

Banks are now competitive with money market mutual funds. They guarantee for one-month periods interest rates tied to the Treasury bill rate or the average money market rate. Bank funds also offer this added attraction: They are federally insured.

Bank money market accounts require depositors to maintain an average monthly balance of $2,500; if the account falls below this minimum, the interest rate is reduced to the passbook rate. Investors are allowed transfers to other accounts and limited checkwriting features. Unlimited checkwriting is available through interest-bearing superNOW accounts which also require a $2,500 average monthly balance. Interest on the superNOW accounts may vary.

The way banks pay interest

Even savings institutions offering maximum interest rates may not follow similar methods of compounding interest. Government regulations call for banks to give new customers full information on interest computation and to advise of any change of system later adopted. Sometimes a hard-pressed savings institution will, for a period, conserve assets by not compounding interest on new accounts. Avoid opening an account during this time.

Sometimes differences in methods of interest computation are not significant. For example, a savings institution might advertise continuous compounding of interest while its competitor offers daily compounding. On $1,000 at 10%, the difference is 8¢ a year. However, the difference is greater between daily compounding and monthly, quarterly, or even annual compounding.

Some banks pay interest only on the lowest balance in an account during an interest period. Others operate complicated systems of offsetting withdrawals against deposits in such a way as to deny the customer the full benefit of interest he thought his account was earning. Note that when 5.5% interest is offered, with an annual yield of 5.73%, the higher rate only applies when the account is left open until the end of the year. If you are moving but not in immediate need of the funds, you should have a final check closing your account sent to you after interest has been posted at the end of the year.

Income tax on interest earned on a short-term certificate may, at a savings institution's option, be deferred. For example, in July, you put $10,000 into a six-month certificate which does not mature until the following year. A bank or thrift may offer a tax-savings plan whereby your simple interest is retained in the account and so is not available until the following tax year. In that case, the Form 1099 issued by the institution at the end of the first year will not show the accumulated interest. You will not owe tax until the year in which you receive the interest.

However, if the bank or thrift offering this option also has a plan whereby the simple interest may be transferred each month to earn interest in your passbook account, you have to consider whether you want the tax-deferral advantage or extra interest. If you do not take a tax-advantage plan, you should be able to withdraw interest at any time whether or not transferred to a passbook account. Not all thrifts offer this option.

Watch maturity dates

Banks and thrifts should notify customers when term deposits are coming due and offer options of payment, renewal, or transfer to other types of accounts. But if you do not give instructions in time, the maturing funds may be transferred to a day-of-deposit account at lower interest, or automatically renewed. On opening an account, you may be asked if you want automatic renewal at maturity, or it may be the institution's policy to set up accounts this way. In periods of fluctuating interest rates, you will want to weigh your options at renewal time.

Financial management accounts

To compete with the rapid growth of insured bank money market funds, brokerage firms developed financial accounts combining a securities management account with checkwriting privileges and a money market fund. As these accounts are now popular, banks and insurance companies also offer them.

In a financial management account, proceeds from securities transactions are automatically transferred to a money-market fund so that idle funds immediately earn interest. Some accounts offer a choice of funds, such as a regular cash fund or a tax-free money market fund.

Brokerage services are provided on either a discounted or full commission basis. Banks generally use discount brokers and may provide larger loans in stock margin accounts than brokerage firms. However, interest charged by banks may be higher than the interest charged by brokerage firms.

Loan terms vary. Some accounts allow margin loans at any time while others provide margin loans only after the balance in your money market account is reduced to zero. Some accounts allow you to write checks that exceed the balance in your money market account; a loan from your margin account covers the excess.

With some financial management accounts, canceled checks are returned automatically. However, many brokerage firms do not return checks but list check numbers and amounts on a monthly statement. To get a canceled check, you must pay a fee.

A financial management account may provide a special statement for keeping track of tax deductible expenses and allow you to enter a code on your checks for tax-deductible items.

If you are interested in a financial management account, shop around for one that provides the services you need at the lowest cost. Some accounts require an initial investment in cash and/or securities of only $1,000; others may require as much as $20,000. Annual fees generally range from $25 to $100. Some firms waive their annual fee if a substantial balance is maintained. These fees are in addition to broker commissions.

The safety of your savings

Wherever placed, be sure your savings have insurance protection. Funds in commercial banks and mutual savings banks are protected through the Federal Deposit Insurance Corporation (FDIC) while the Federal Savings and Loan Insurance Corporation (FSLIC) guarantees deposits in savings and loan associations. In some states, savings are protected by state insurance agencies. The current federal ceiling on coverage is $100,000 for an individual at each savings institution; you can have more coverage if you open accounts in several institutions and do not exceed $100,000 at any one. You can also increase your coverage at each institution by having more than one type of account. A couple or family can arrange for more than $100,000 in coverage by using joint accounts, testamentary revocable trust accounts, and irrevocable trust accounts. Each type of account is separately insured up to the $100,000 ceiling. Individual retirement accounts (IRAs) are separately insured up to $100,000. Congress may raise this IRA limit to $250,000.

Wherever placed, be sure your savings have insurance protection.

In the case of a bank or thrift failure, customers receive their funds plus interest within a week or ten days. However, in most recent cases of failure, a merger has been arranged so that a stronger institution takes over and an insurance payout is not necessary.

United States Savings Bonds

Savings bonds backed by the credit of the United States government continue to play a role in the financial security plans of millions of American families; more than $68 billion worth of these securities is currently outstanding. In addition

to patriotic reasons, investors have been attracted to savings
bonds for one or more of these reasons:

1. United States Series EE bonds can be redeemed at a stated
   value on demand after six months from the issue date, HH
   bonds after six months but with a penalty.
2. These bonds have been a "liquid" reserve, quickly and
   easily translated into dollars and cents when needed. Only
   EE bonds will have this feature in the future. Penalties
   apply in the case of HH bonds.
3. Savings bonds are not subject to market fluctuations; they
   are never redeemed for less than the amount invested.
4. Interest on savings bonds is not subject to state or local
   income or personal property taxes.
5. The federal income tax on Series E bonds and EE bonds
   interest can be deferred; the annual increases in value need
   not be reported until the bond is cashed.
6. If savings bonds are lost, stolen, or destroyed, they can be
   replaced without cost.
7. Savings bonds are easy and convenient to buy. They are
   sold at neighborhood banks and savings institutions. Also,
   many corporations have payroll savings plans through
   which an employee can buy bonds regularly by authoriz-
   ing automatic paycheck deductions.

To make savings bonds more competitive with other current savings opportunities, the Treasury offers EE bonds
which, if held for at least five years, earn a variable rate of
interest equal to 85% of the average return on five-year Treasury securities. To protect against a sharp downturn in Treasury securities rates, a minimum rate of 7.5% for EE bonds
is guaranteed for the five-year period. EE bonds cashed before five years yield a lower fixed rate, based on the holding
period of the bond. The variable rate is recalculated every
six months based on sales of Treasury securities. Bonds purchased before November 1, 1982 which are held beyond
October 1987 also qualify for the variable rate if that rate is
higher than the guaranteed rate in effect when the bonds were
purchased.

On the other hand, there are disadvantages to savings bonds
as a form of investment:

1. Savings bonds cannot be used as collateral and cannot be pledged. If money is needed, the bonds must be cashed and an immediate tax incurred not only on the current, but also on the accumulated, interest on which tax has been deferred.

2. Compared to other investments, such as securities or real estate, savings bonds do not offer growth potential. The lack of growth potential, coupled with inflation, is considered the greatest disadvantage of savings bonds as an investment.

Types of savings bonds

Series E and Series H bonds were sold until January 1, 1980. They have now been replaced by Series EE and Series HH bonds. All the bonds are described below.

Series E bonds. This is the most widely held bond; it was sold at 75% of face value, maturing in five years from the date of issue.

Series E bonds can be cashed in at most banks prior to maturity. No notice is required. These bonds are not negotiable and cannot be used as collateral for loans. They must be in registered form. Registration may be in the name of a single owner, adult or minor, with or without beneficiary, or in co-ownership form.

Previously, holders of E bonds could obtain ten-year extensions on maturity. Now, E bonds bought from 1941 to April 1952 on which extensions have been granted come to final maturity between 1981 and April 1992, forty years after issuance. No more interest will be paid, but holders have the option of redeeming and paying tax due on the accumulated interest or continuing deferral by exchanging them for HH bonds. Series E bonds issued after April 1952 are allowed another ten-year extension. Series E bonds purchased in 1979 can earn interest for up to 25 years.

Below is a list of final maturity dates for E bonds, beyond which no interest will accrue:

Date of issue	Date of maturity	Term of bond
May 1941–Apr. 1952	May 1981–Apr. 1992	40 years
May 1952–Jan. 1957	Jan. 1992–Sept. 1996	39 years, 8 mos.
Feb. 1957–May 1959	Jan. 1996–Apr. 1998	38 years, 11 mos.
June 1959–Nov. 1965	Mar. 1997–Aug. 2003	37 years, 9 mos.
Dec. 1965–May 1969	Dec. 1992–May 1996	27 years
June 1969–Nov. 1973	Apr. 1995–Sept. 1999	25 years, 10 mos.
Dec. 1973–June 1980	Dec. 1998–June 2005	25 years

Final maturity dates for H bonds are as follows:

Date of issue	Date of maturity	Term of bond
June 1952–Jan. 1957	Feb. 1982–Sept. 1986	29 years, 8 mos.
Feb. 1957–May 1959	Feb. 1987–May 1989	30 years
June 1959–Dec. 1979	June 1989–Dec. 2009	30 years

Series H bonds. The H bond was sold in denominations of $500, $1,000, $5,000, and $10,000, maturing ten years from its issue date and paying interest semiannually. This bond is priced at par or face value and is redeemable at par.

Interest ends on Series H bonds bought before July 1959 and which mature between February 1982 and May 1989. These old bonds must be cashed at maturity. However, H bonds bought after June 1959 are allowed one more ten-year extension on maturity. ·Up to 3 years is allowed on H bonds purchased in 1979. Series H bonds are not exchangeable for the new HH bonds.

Series EE bonds. EE bonds sell in denominations of $50 through $10,000, with the annual accumulation set at $15,000. Because the price is half the face amount, a $50 EE bond costs $25. The waiting time until maturity is 11 years and 9 months, with a ten-year extension allowed.

Series HH bonds. HH bonds are no longer available except by exchanging EE or older E bonds. HH bonds are issued in denominations of $500, $1,000, $5,000, and $10,000 and pay interest semiannually.

Naming beneficiaries. On Series E and Series H bonds, the beneficiary must agree if the buyer wishes to name another person to inherit. If refused, the buyer's only way to change the beneficiary is to cash in the bond and buy a new one. For all the bonds, the owner retains control during his lifetime. Buyers of EE bonds may change or delete the name of a beneficiary without notifying such a person (or persons) and obtaining consent to do so.

Tax aspects of savings bonds. The exchange of maturing Series E bonds into Series H bonds was a popular device over the years to defer the payment of tax on the E bonds. An older person could legally avoid E bond interest tax until death, when his or her estate would have to pay. Holders of E bonds may now exchange them for Series HH bonds. This exchange will continue to defer tax on the interest of the E bonds until the HH bonds are redeemed or mature. The semiannual interest on HH bonds is subject to federal income tax, but not to state and local taxes.

Series E and EE bondholders may decide not to defer payment of tax on interest but report the increase in the bond's value each year. If you have accumulated bonds for some years without paying tax and make the decision to pay annually, you may elect to do so by including all the accumulated interest on which tax has been postponed. But once you have made such an election, you need approval of the Treasury before changing that method of reporting.

Interest on checking accounts

There are now ways in which interest can be earned on checking accounts, but not all bank customers do or should take advantage of the opportunity. Interest-bearing checking accounts come in several varieties according to the banks or thrifts which issue them, and it is not easy to decide which may be advantageous.

The first type of interest-bearing checking account is the Negotiable Order of Withdrawal (NOW). Though NOW accounts were previously restricted by law to banks and thrifts in certain states, they are now offered throughout the country. Banks began offering Authorized Transfer Service (ATS) in 1978, but many abandoned ATS in favor of the NOW system.

Negotiable Order of Withdrawal (NOW) accounts. Initially, these interest-bearing checking accounts operated at no charge, but expenses caused the imposition of minimum balances. If the average balance falls below the minimum, you must pay a service charge for that month. Technically, negotiable orders of withdrawal are not checks but operate in the same way. Check for any restrictions that may apply.

Sweep accounts. Savings institutions have begun offering a variation of a NOW account, called a sweep account. The account operates as a NOW account, but you may earn higher interest because funds above a specified minimum are "swept" into a money market fund. At some institutions, money is swept into a bank repurchase agreement (repo). The transfer is often automatic, though at some institutions you have to request it by telephone or in person. There may be a fee for this service, or you may have to pay a fee only if the balance falls below the minimum.

To some depositors, the convenience of a sweep account may make it worthwhile. However, if you keep track of your checking and are seeking high interest, it would be more profitable to invest separately in a money market fund or other instrument. Note that funds invested in money market funds, even through a sweep account, are not federally insured.

In general, anyone who has been keeping a high balance in a non-interest-bearing checking account may benefit by switching to an ATS or NOW account.

Authorized Transfer Service (ATS). You may never see this term if you go to a bank offering the service. Banks may label their own ATS offerings with special names. The customer has both a checking and a savings account; funds may be kept in the interest-bearing savings account until needed when they are automatically transferred into the checking account, or you may arrange to have a specified amount deducted regularly from the checking account and deposited in the savings account. Banks and thrifts usually impose minimum balances for savings, from $500 upward, often $2,000 or $3,000; some have transfer fees, some check fees. Usually fees apply if the balance falls below the minimum.

Should you use an interest-bearing checking account? In general, anyone who has been keeping a high balance in a non-interest-bearing checking account may benefit by switching to an ATS or NOW account. But customers in the habit of maintaining a low balance and writing many checks may find that fees and penalties for dropping below the minimum may outstrip the interest earned, especially after taxes on the interest are considered. If, at a financial institution in your area, a low minimum balance is required for a NOW or ATS account, and any fees and charges are reasonable, the convenience of such a plan may make it advantageous.

Nevertheless, many people like the old separate system for the good reason that they intend savings for future use and use checking accounts to pay bills. They prefer not to mix the two.

Special checking account plans for senior citizens

Many banks and thrifts offer advantageous checking account terms to senior citizens, sometimes in association with the automatic deposit of Social Security checks. Some financial institutions call for the establishment of a minimum savings account as well as the checking account; some do not require it.

The definition of "senior citizen" may vary. In some areas age 60 qualifies an individual for senior privileges; elsewhere it may be age 62 or age 65. Senior citizens, whether working or not, should inquire at banks and thrifts about no-fee or low-cost checking.

Do not neglect your account

A little-publicized fact is that savings accounts dormant for a number of years may cease earning interest. Also, every state practices escheat, that is, seizure of property with no apparent owner. One of the most common forms of escheat is acquisition by the state of unclaimed savings deposits.

Depending on the state in which the savings institution is located, an account that has been dormant for a number of years becomes vulnerable to the laws of escheat. If a financial institution fails to reach a depositor through the mails at the last known address or through advertisements and public notices, it must turn the funds over to a state after its defined number of years, sometimes five or ten, has elapsed. Once the money has been handed over to the state, getting it back is an involved procedure.

To safeguard your savings, you should keep a record of all your accounts and their numbers with the names and addresses of the financial institutions. At least once a year have interest entered in each account book you have. If you move, give your address to every institution in which you have an account.

Part III. CHOOSING THE RIGHT INVESTMENT FOR YOU

Now that you are familiar with interest income options available in the money market and savings institutions, how do you choose the right vehicle for you? Many factors will affect your decision. Here are important points to consider.

How much money do you have to invest? The amount you are planning to invest will limit the types of investments open to you. If you have only $100 or $200 now, most high-yielding investments are out of your reach. Only certain bank instruments and accounts and EE bonds have such minimums. If you have $1,000 to invest, more options become available in addition to bank instruments and savings banks. Some money market funds have $1,000 minimum investments. Unit investment trusts typically have $1,000 per unit requirements. Certain Treasury bonds and notes also require only a $1,000 minimum investment. Similarly, obligations of U.S. agencies purchased as units of certificates (for example, Government National Mortgage Association [GNMA] pass-throughs) can be bought for $1,000. If you have $5,000 to invest, many investments besides those already mentioned are open to you. You can pick from almost any money market fund (only certain tax-exempt funds have larger minimums). Corporate bonds and tax-exempt bonds are usually sold in $5,000 denominations. A minimum may be required for bank certificates of deposit (CD). A $10,000 investment is required for a Treasury bill. Certain U.S. agency obligations and tax-exempt notes require an investment of $25,000.

How long can you tie up your money? Consider your personal commitments for which money will be required in the future, as well as your expectations for interest-rate fluctuation. Do you need your money in six months, or can you afford to tie up your funds for 20 years? Even if you can commit funds long term, you may think interest rates will rise and therefore do not wish to be locked into lower returns. When you have answered the question of how long you can tie up your money, certain investment options will suggest themselves. For the long term, there are corporate and tax-exempt bonds in which interest is guaranteed for periods of as much as 20 years or more. Treasury bonds have maturities exceeding ten years. Unit trust investments typically run long term but can be sold at any time (although principal may be sacrificed if interest rates at the time of sale are higher than when the units were bought). Many bank obligations have intermediate maturities of 18 or 30 months. Treasury bills as well as six-month bank CDs have a six-month maturity. Most banks are also offering short-term accounts or CDs, such as the 91-day CD, and 8- to 89-day repos. For an investment without a fixed maturity, money market funds and other mutual funds are also available.

For those seeking safety, bank obligations insured by the FDIC or FSLIC and Treasury obligations backed by the full faith and credit of the United States government are the best choice.

How much are you willing to risk on your investment? You must decide how much of a risk you can take with your investment. If it is money needed for a specific purpose, a down payment on a home or a college fund, you should be concerned with safety. If you have money with which you wish to speculate, you may foresake safety in favor of a higher return. As a general rule, the price of safety is a lower return than could be received from a comparable but less secure investment. For those seeking safety, bank obligations insured by the FDIC or FSLIC and Treasury obligations backed by the full faith and credit of the United States government are the best choice. The safety of other investments is not guaranteed but can be evaluated through financial rating services. All investments involve some element of risk. Even if your principal is guaranteed, as with a Treasury obligation, you cannot foresee future interest rates.

What is your tax bracket and investment portfolio? Tax considerations and your other holdings will affect your choice of investments. For those in the top tax bracket, tax-exempt investments are favored because the return will usually be better than taxable investments after tax savings is taken into account. Treasury obligations offer the investor a return free from state and local tax. The extent of savings will vary with your bracket and state tax laws.

Your other investments will also affect how you invest for interest income. If you have a portfolio of blue-chip stocks, you may wish to take more risk with high-yielding interest obligations. Conversely, if you speculate in the stock market, you may wish to balance your holdings by investing in safer interest obligations.

Chapter 3

INVESTING IN THE STOCK MARKET

STOCK market investments offer the opportunity to increase your capital investment which, upon a sale, will be taxed at favorable capital gain rates, and to receive current income in the form of dividends. Some stocks may offer only small dividends or none at all, emphasizing growth potential instead. Other stocks, such as blue chips, produce a steady income but have less prospect for capital gain. Which type of stocks to invest in, or whether to invest at all, are decisions you must base on your personal and financial situation.

This chapter will acquaint you with stock market terminology, help you appraise the risks of investing, and assist you in choosing a broker. High-risk investments, such as commodity futures, are not discussed since these ventures are best left to sophisticated investors and speculators. Investments in mutual funds and investment clubs are discussed later in this chapter.

What are securities?

If stock market investments are new to you, read the following section carefully. You need to know the difference between

61

common stock and preferred stock, and the difference between stocks and bonds.

Stock. When you buy shares of stock of a corporation, you are investing money in that company; in a sense, you become a part owner. In return for your investment, the corporation generally pays you dividends out of its earnings and profits. If the corporation is successful, the value of your shares of stock may increase. Any increase in the value of your shares is not taxable until you sell them. On the other hand, if the corporation does poorly, you may receive few or no dividends and your shares of stock may decline in value. Other factors including general economic conditions and public confidence affect your stock; your shares may decline in value even though the company itself is making money and growing.

There are two categories of stock, common and preferred. In the case of preferred stock, dividends are usually set at a fixed amount. The claims of preferred stockholders come after company bondholders and take precedence over those of common stockholders. Thus if the company goes bankrupt or liquidates, bondholders' claims on the company's assets come before those of preferred stockholders. The interest due on the company's bonds takes precedence over the dividends on its preferred stock. Claims of common stockholders come last. Holders of common stock participate in the concern's profits or losses via fluctuating dividends.

When you buy shares of stock of a corporation, you are investing money in that company; in a sense, you become a part owner.

The preferred stock of one company may be a "safer" investment in terms of assets and earnings than the bonds of another company. Usually high-grade preferred stock provides a steadier dividend income than common stocks. Common stocks, on the other hand, offer greater opportunity for appreciation.

Convertible securities. Convertible securities are issued in preferred stock or bond form. They are called convertibles because the preferred stock or bonds can be converted into common stock of the issuing company at the election of the investor. Common stock is never convertible into another type of security. As a rule, the convertible privilege is written on the bond or preferred stock certificate. There are some issues, however, which are convertible as a result of a detachable warrant issued with the security, usually a bond.

Conversion privileges and terms vary with the particular security. The convertible preferred of one company might be convertible into one share of its common stock, while that of another company might be convertible into three shares of its common stock. Also, the conversion privilege might continue indefinitely or be limited to a period of time ending on a specified date.

Investors often choose convertible securities for capital gains and as a hedge against market decline.

Investors often choose convertible securities for capital gains and as a hedge against market decline. As a convertible security is either a bond or preferred stock, it has a senior position in the company's capitalization before common stockholders are paid off. If the stock market drops, these securities are sometimes less vulnerable to the decline. Thus danger of a large capital loss is lessened. Since the convertible security can be converted into the common stock, its value moves up as the value of the common rises.

A convertible generally will command a premium over and above its intrinsic worth. You must pay something for the conversion privilege.

Stock rights. Stock rights give stockholders the first opportunity to buy new securities the company issues to raise money. Each stockholder receives a rights certificate to buy new securities in proportion to the number of shares already owned. Stockholders are allowed to buy the new securities at a below-market price. Because of this value, rights themselves can be sold and traded. Rights are only good for a short, specified period. The stockholder who lets a rights certificate expire loses because (1) the certificate could have been sold at a profit, and (2) with the new shares in the company, the stockholder's holdings are now proportionately less.

Warrants. Warrants are also rights to buy, but they usually come with stocks or bonds as a package when purchased and are good for a few years. Like rights certificates, some warrants are also traded separately. The value of this feature depends on your expectations of the securities' performance.

Puts and calls. You may purchase options to buy and sell stock. On the stock exchange these options are referred to as calls and puts. A *call* gives you the right to require the seller of the option to sell you stock at a fixed price for a specified period. A *put* gives you the right to require the seller of the option to buy stock you own at a fixed price during the option period.

You may buy puts and calls to speculate on stock prices or to hedge your stock holdings. If you believe the price of stock you own will fall, you can buy a put to limit your losses in case of a decline. If you expect the price to rise, you may buy a call enabling you to buy more stock in the future at a price agreed to now.

You do not have to exercise puts and calls to make a profit. Instead you may sell them to other investors because the value of options fluctuates with the stocks.

Trading in options is highly speculative, attracting those who hope to make profits on minimum investments. It is not an investment area for market novices.

Puts and calls allow you to speculate at the expense of a small investment; the price of the option is much lower than the cost of buying shares of stock. The price of the option depends on the value of the stock, the length of the option period, the volatility of the stock, and the demand and supply for options for the particular stock.

Exchange option trading. Option market exchanges have

standardized market conditions for trading in put and call options. However, the overwhelming number of options transacted are calls; the trading of puts is currently limited. Financial sections of daily newspapers provide data on the market prices and volume of the options.

Option markets are the Chicago Board of Exchange, the American Exchange, the Philadelphia Stock Exchange, the Midwest Exchange, and the Pacific Stock Exchange.

Trading in options is highly speculative, attracting those who hope to make profits on minimum investments. It is not an investment area for market novices. For institutions holding large portfolios, options trading hedges their market position and earns income through the sale of options based on their holdings.

Stock market risks

There is no guarantee that the companies in which you invest will meet your investment objectives. The stock of even the largest companies has been known to succumb to price erosion. When dealing with stocks, keep in mind that it is impossible to avoid risk even in the seemingly safest of situations. Day-to-day fluctuations in the market or in the price of an individual stock are almost impossible to predict. These are only a few of the hazards of stock ownership, which cannot be stressed too strongly to the novice investor.

Unfortunately, there is no way to eliminate investment risk; no reliable means have been found to predict future economic trends. You must be prepared to see the value of your stock decline as well as rise. During critical periods, the atmosphere surrounding stock market investment is charged with fear and apprehension. Panic selling may take place, sending stock prices down sharply. As a potential investor you must consider your own emotional makeup. If you cannot operate under conditions of stress, then the stock market is not for you.

The stock market is a highly complex field and demands patient study. Few stocks, if any, are so safe that they can be purchased and then left unadministered. You can minimize risk only by constant supervision of your investments. Also, get the best advice you can. If you have a broker who has satisfied you in the past, rely on his or her judgment. If you have had no experience in security investment, read the literature published by the large investment houses and choose a broker you feel will best serve your purposes. Tips on choosing a broker are discussed later in this chapter.

Can you afford stock market risk?

Before you start planning an investment program, you must decide how much of a cash reserve you will need to retain for emergencies and current obligations. A comfortable cash reserve should be kept in savings accounts, money market funds, or in easily converted investments such as government bonds.
Also weigh the following:

1. Have you income from other sources or will your investment returns be a major source of funds for day-to-day living expenses?
2. What is your need for the cash you are investing? Can you afford to keep it invested indefinitely? You may need the money at a fixed time, in which case you must restrict yourself to safe and marketable securities which can generally be converted to cash at any time.

Fixing your investment objectives

Before selecting securities to buy, you must also decide what you want and need from your investments. Do you want stock that will return dividends every few months and will be rela-

---

High income, high profits, high stability, and high liquidity do not come in one package.

---

tively stable in price and quality? Do you want a high-income security to cover part of your living expenses? Is your objective the sale of the stock at a substantially higher price than you paid for it? Are you concerned with liquidity and market-ability because you will need cash suddenly for some business or personal purpose and you want to be sure you can sell at a price approximating your cost whenever the need arises?

If your objective is "trading" profits, you will generally have to deal in stocks that are fairly risky and which fluctuate widely in price. If liquidity is your aim, you will have to buy stocks of the highest grade that fluctuate only slightly in price. High income, high profits, high stability, and high liquidity do not come in one package.

Decide on your objective or objectives. As a guide, here are some suggestions to consider:

1. Invest in sound, essential industries. Food and utilities are basic industries and more readily hold their values during economic declines than nonessential industries that provide services and luxuries. Of course, all essential industries must be watched and attention paid to any trend that might suggest a particular industry is becoming replaced or outmoded by new technological developments.
2. Invest in companies that are recognized leaders in their industries. True, some analysts do not agree with this advice and hold that the only substantial profits are made in new, unknown companies. But you are investing, not trying to "get rich quick." Some smaller companies may turn out to be more profitable than well-known firms; but the chance of choosing such a company is often a matter of luck. The advantages in selecting recognized companies is that they have proven their ability to survive, their management is experienced, they will have resources for research, and they can finance their needs more easily than smaller companies.
3. Invest in several different companies, each in a different industry. Over a period of time you undoubtedly will make a bad investment. If you invest in only one company, an error may be costly; if you have, say, six different stocks, your good judgment on four of them may more than offset a bad decision on one or two. Of course, you may also "hedge" in the same way by investing in mutual funds.

4. Invest about the same amount in the shares of each company you select. Do not make a favorite of any one stock. There are many sound industries.

5. Invest in shares listed on a major securities exchange, preferably the New York Stock Exchange. Before its stock may be listed on a major exchange, a company must file information with both the private financial authorities and the federal government. Specific standards must be met; regular reports must be published; transactions are under the constant check of the exchange, the federal government, the Securities and Exchange Commission (SEC), and expert investors and bankers. Furthermore, a listing on the exchange makes it easier to buy or sell stock. Listing, of course, is no guarantee of merit, but it is a likely indication that the company will operate according to current business standards.

6. Invest in shares that can show an unbroken earnings or dividend record or both for the last ten years. Such a record indicates that an enterprise is sound.

7. Buy shares that over the past ten years have earned at least five dollars for every four paid out in dividends. A company should not pay out all it earns, but should build up a reserve to handle emergencies or to ensure its ability to take advantage of future opportunities. A company that earns considerably more than its dividend is preferred to one that just earns it.

8. During a period of a year or two, sell at least one stock, choosing the weakest on your list without considering the original cost. Invest the proceeds in a more profitable security.

9. Do not hesitate to cut your losses. If a stock declines substantially or shows a fundamental problem, for example, an extended decline in sales, sell before you lose even more of your investment. On the other hand, if the price–earnings ratio rises sharply within a short period, that too may be an indication to sell. If a stock becomes overvalued, you should sell to receive your maximum profit.

10. When you place an order to buy or sell, do not set a fixed price; buy or sell "at the market." Buying or selling at the market means that your order will be filled at about the

price of the next transaction in your stock on the exchange. This is a better approach than giving your broker a fixed price. You are a long-term investor, and even an expert cannot fix the value of a stock to within fractions of a point. Since you are investing for the long term, it will be unimportant over that period whether you paid $20 or $21 for a specific share of stock.

11. Do not buy on margin. This involves borrowing money from your broker to buy new securities and using your stock as collateral. Buying on margin is expensive, especially when interest rates are high. Brokers borrow money from banks to lend to their customers. They charge customers from ½ % to 1½ % more than the rate paid to the bank. In addition, buying on margin is very risky. If the price of the stock falls, the broker will demand either more money or the sale of the stock—at a loss.

12. If you do buy on margin, you should check the fine points of your agreement and understand the rights retained by your broker. You may have to notify him if you want to prevent his taking certain buy-and-sell actions. The broker wants to save paperwork; his rights may not always suit your plans. Stock bought on margin must remain with your broker and is registered in the name of the brokerage firm ("in street name").

13. Brokers find it easier to hold the stock of small investors in street name. You may have to insist that your stock be registered in your name. Customers are now insured to $500,000 against brokerage house insolvency. If you deal with more than one firm, or if a husband and wife maintain separate and joint accounts with one broker, each account is insured for $500,000. Some brokerage houses offer additional insurance protection against the loss of securities and cash in their keeping. There is, of course, no insurance against stock market loss.

When to buy stocks

A review of the stock market's history indicates that there is a cyclical pattern to prices. However, the trouble is that market lows and highs stand out clearly only in retrospect.

Charts which show "where the market has been" do not necessarily show where it is going. True, experts study the current market to determine whether it is advisable to buy or sell at current market prices and to predict the future moves of a particular stock. But for the average investor, market analysts suggest "Give up any idea of beating the market." The retiree, in particular, will want to develop a conservative investment program.

If appropriate to your circumstances, you can use such approaches as dollar cost averaging or a plan suggested by a brokerage house.

Charts which show "where the market has been" do not necessarily show where it is going.

Dollar cost averaging. In a dollar cost averaging program you periodically invest a fixed amount in the same stock (every month or quarter). Your money buys more shares when prices are low and fewer when prices are high. However, if the price is on a down cycle, you are merely buying an increasing number of shares of a declining stock. If the stock price is on the upswing, buying during the temporary decline lowers the average price of your holdings, thereby increasing the potential gain, assuming the stock goes up again. Of course, if you have to unload the stock during a bearish (declining) market, you will come out a loser. To be sure, if you could have afforded to keep buying the low-cost shares, you might later have made a profit since the possibility also exists that the stock will go up. Company bankruptcies are also a risk.

Regular investment plans. If you are a new investor interested in a plan for gradual investments on a budget, you can obtain information at the New York Stock Exchange which lists member firms offering such plans.

Information about investments

To reduce the element of risk, familiarize yourself with services available to the investor. Here are sources of important data on investing:

1. The Department of Public Information, New York Stock Exchange, 11 Wall Street, New York, NY 10005. You may write for a list of member firms which will guide you to brokers who handle your type of account. The office gives general information helpful to the small investor and to the newcomer to the stock market. Inquire about the "Investor's Information Kit," a useful guide, available at low cost.

2. The financial sections of newspapers and the publications of concerns specializing in financial developments. Several long-established, respected financial services operate throughout the country; they summarize basic news. These are available to any subscriber in any town or city. Many libraries have copies of the *Wall Street Journal,* the *New York Times, Barron's, Forbes,* and other periodicals giving financial news.

3. The companies themselves. If you write to a company whose stock you may be interested in buying, you can obtain an annual report and prospectus which will give you information about the company.

4. Stockbrokers. Many brokerage firms maintain large research departments and many have branches throughout the country. They can be a valuable source of information.

5. Investment advisory services. Unless you have a substantial amount to invest, they are probably not for you. Their fees for weekly and monthly reports are considerable.

6. Investment counsel firms. These firms charge fixed fees for their advice and are prepared to manage a client's complete investment portfolio. The larger firms usually do not accept clients with small accounts.

Reading the prospectus and annual report

A company's prospectus and annual report are useful tools for the potential investor; however, some knowledge is required to make sense of the figures presented.

The Securities and Exchange Commission requires public companies to print a prospectus disclosing certain information. However, the SEC does not endorse or investigate each company. Every prospectus carries the SEC disclaimer: "These securities have not been approved or disapproved by the Securities and Exchange Commission nor has the Commission passed upon the accuracy of this prospectus. Any representation to the contrary is a criminal offense."

When reading the prospectus, consider the company's objectives and how it is managed. How big is the company? Look at the assets in the balance sheet. Size is an indication of stability since larger companies have less risk of sudden failure. Age is also a factor of stability. A company that has made it through the first few rough years is a better bet than one just starting out.

Good management is critical to the success of a company. The prospectus lists the officers of the company and their experience or affiliations. To obtain more information on these individuals, you can check back issues of business periodicals. The prospectus should say how many shares are owned by management. Are the officers of the company investing personally in what they hope you will invest in? If they own a substantial number of shares, look under "dilution" to see if they bought them at prices much lower than the going rate. The prospectus lists salaries for management. Consider these figures in terms of percentage of company earnings.

Investors tend to look at earnings first when reading a prospectus or annual report. To get a better idea of company performance, compare this figure with previous years' earnings. Also, check the company's profit margin, computed by dividing the net income figure for the year by the sales for the year. If you are willing to do more research, you can look up industry averages at the library to see how this company stands in relation to others in the same business. Services such as Value Line and Standard & Poors are helpful.

Turn to the auditor's report which should establish that the statements are presented according to generally accepted accounting principles.

A prime indicator of the company's strength is its debt-equity ratio.

When checking profits, look for "extraordinary," i.e., not continual, items that may only affect profits this year. A change in accounting methods can also alter results. Extraordinary items or a change in accounting methods should be noted in footnotes. Read all auditor's footnotes carefully; they contain important information.

A prime indicator of the company's strength is its debt–equity ratio. Divide the total shareholders' equity by the total long-term debt. The higher this figure is, the more the company relies on its creditors and can be affected by them. Debt is not considered excessive if a bank or other commercial lending institution would be satisfied with the terms of the debt instruments and the corporation's overall financial structure. Debt is also not considered excessive if the debt–equity ratio does not exceed 10:1.

Financial reports usually include a letter from the president or chairman of the board. These letters tend to be very positive, but they may also discuss problems the company is experiencing, its current financial health, and plans for the future.

Reading the financial pages of the newspaper

When you buy stocks, you will want to keep abreast of how your holdings are doing. To do this, you should be able to scan the stock market listings. Here is a brief explanation of how to read the financial tables in your newspaper.

Stocks are listed according to the exchange on which they are traded, such as the New York Stock Exchange, the American Stock Exchange, and Over-the-Counter. Below is an excerpt from the listing for the New York Stock Exchange. Each stock listed has its own code or abbreviation. If you are uncertain of your stock's designation, check with your broker. The example below is "Eskod," or Eastman Kodak.

52-week		Stock	Div	Yld %	PE Ratio	Sales 100s	High	Low	Last	Chg.
High	Low									
85⅜	60⅝	Eskod	3.00a	4.2	9	3594	72⅜	71⅛	72¼	+¾

Prices are quoted as fractions of a dollar. For example, 14½ means $14.50; 28⅜ means $28.38. The first two columns show the highest price and lowest price for which the stock traded during the past 52 weeks (including the current week but not the current day). Thus, for Kodak, its high was 85⅜ or $85.38 and its low was 60⅝ or $60.63.

The column after the name of the stock shows the annual dividends based on the most recent quarterly or semiannual dividend declaration. For Kodak, the 3.00 means that for each share of stock, $3 is the annual dividend. Since Kodak pays its dividends quarterly, the most recent quarterly dividend was 75¢ per share. The "a" following the dividend means that extra dividends or payments were made.

The next column is the stock's yield, a percentage arrived at by dividing the dividend by the closing price. Kodak's yield is 4.2 (the dividend of $3 ÷ 72¼).

The column after the yield is the PE (price/earnings) ratio of the stock which is the price of the stock divided by the earnings per share. The earnings are not listed. Kodak's PE ratio is 9.

The next column shows the number of shares traded for the day. The listing is in hundreds. For Kodak, the 3594 entry means that 359,400 shares were traded.

The last three columns before the plus or minus sign show the day's trading. The first of these columns shows how high the stock was traded; the next column, how low the stock was traded; and the last of these columns, what the stock "closed at," or the final trading price. The plus or minus sign indicates whether the closing price is higher or lower than the preceding day's closing price. If there is no plus or minus sign, the stock's closing price was unchanged from the preceding day's closing price. The last fraction shows this differential. For Kodak, its highest trading price was 72⅜ or $72.38; its lowest was 71⅛ or $71.13. It closed at 72¼ or $72.25. This price was +¾, or up 75¢ from the previous day's closing price of $71.50.

Other codes that may follow prices or dividends are explained in a legend on the financial page.

Choosing a broker

When you have sufficient capital to begin your investment program, you will probably want to use the services of a broker. Your plans and the size of your holdings will determine which broker is best for you.

Choose an established brokerage firm. Ask whether it is a

member of the National Association of Securities Dealers and of which exchanges it is a member.

If you require a broker only to place buy and sell orders, you can save on commissions by using a discount broker. On a simple transaction, the discount can be as much as 75% of a regular broker's commission. Also, with the expansion of the discount business, some firms provide margin accounts, telephone orders, and stock quotes outside regular business hours, discounted subscriptions to financial publications, and money market funds for idle cash.

On the other hand, if you want expert advice, you should consult a regular broker. The large brokerage firms may offer attractive packages. However, others may not welcome small accounts.

If you require a broker only to place buy and sell orders, you can save on commissions by using a discount broker. On a simple transaction, the discount can be as much as 75% of a regular broker's commission.

Go to several brokerage firms before deciding on one. Meet the brokers in person. Visiting firms enables you to meet a few brokers at each and to select one in whom you have confidence. Do not be afraid to ask questions. Inquire about the broker's education, experience, and area of expertise. You will find that not all brokers are equally knowledgable about the various investment options. You may ask for references from his or her clients.

You have no obligation to accept the first broker the firm's office manager assigns to you. He or she may be the person selected by the firm to handle new accounts that day or week, and may not be the most qualified to handle your investment needs. Talking with several people will help you decide if you are more comfortable with an experienced broker, or with an individual who has just completed the firm's training program and who may be more aware of the latest developments.

Avoid telephone solicitations for your account, especially

if the broker is pushing an immediate investment in a "solid deal."

Be aware that the broker's commission depends on the amount and types of securities you invest in. Some forethought about your investment goals helps you to avoid a broker's push in a direction that will earn him or her a large commission without regard to your wishes.

Discuss the nature of the future contact you wish to have with your broker. Decide in advance at what point you want to be advised of changes in the performance of your investments. You want to be informed of "tips" only if they are in line with your investment goals.

Problems with your broker

If you are unhappy with your broker's handling of your account and the two of you are unable to settle your differences, speak to the office manager about the problem. Perhaps your account can be transferred to another broker. If the brokerage firm does not resolve the matter, write to one of the following:

1. For firms that are members of the New York Stock Exchange: Investor–Broker Liaison Section of the New York Stock Exchange, 55 Water Street, New York, NY 10041.
2. For firms belonging to the American Stock Exchange: Rulings and Inquiries Department, American Stock Exchange, 86 Trinity Place, New York, NY 10006.
3. For firms that do not belong to either the NYSE or ASE: National Association of Securities Dealers, 77 Water Street, New York, NY 10005.

Asset management accounts

Your brokerage firm or other financial institution may offer you a universal account or asset management account which combines your stock transactions and other financial services in one centralized account. These accounts are currently offered or planned by stockbrokers, banks, retailers, and insurance companies.

Merrill Lynch created the first asset management account in 1977, and it became the model for others. Its Cash Management Account (CMA) requires a minimum deposit of $20,000 in cash or securities, and features check writing, use of a debit or credit card, and reinvestment of dividends and any other cash into money market funds. The customer enjoys the use of his cash plus market earnings and the borrowing value of his securities. When the CMA customer writes a check, the amount is withdrawn from the checking account, but if more money is needed, it is automatically withdrawn from the money market fund. If the cash and money market shares do not cover the check, Merrill Lynch gives the customer a loan using the securities as collateral. The customer may borrow up to half the market value of marginable stocks in his or her account, but the interest rate is high compared to other consumer credit.

The CMA offers this advantage: if cash is building up in the checking account, it will be deposited in the money market fund to earn interest. Dividends and interest on securities and profits from sales of securities will also be invested in money market shares.

While asset management accounts make some financial transactions more convenient, they do not yet cover all needs. For example, the CMA prospectus advises customers not to use this account to replace a regular checking account. If the CMA checking account is used only for major purchases, there is less paperwork for the company, and it is less confusing for the customer. Check writing and imprinting are free, and there is usually no minimum amount per check. There is an annual fee for the CMA account. The VISA card provided with a CMA is not intended as a general purchase card; it is a debit card for withdrawing money from the account. Some asset management accounts provide credit cards instead of, or in addition to, a debit card. Debit cards do not give the customer the benefit of credit card "float." (See Chapter 4.)

Each month, the customer receives a statement showing assets owned, interest earned and paid, dividends received, brokerage commissions paid, and transactions on the checking account and debit or credit cards.

If you are interested in an asset management account, check the programs offered by banks and brokers and read their prospectuses. Your most important question should be: "Is this account really a convenience for me?"

Asset management accounts have attracted many customers and will be offered more widely in the future. Small investors will be able to use accounts offered by discount brokers. They offer some of the same services but for minimum deposits much lower than required by the large brokers.

If you are interested in an asset management account, check the programs offered by banks and brokers and read their prospectuses. Your most important question should be: "Is this account really a convenience for me?" You can obtain the same basic services separately. Will having them combined in one account simplify your finances? Fees and services will vary with each plan. Some items to ask about are:

1. Minimum deposit requirement.
2. Uses of debit or credit cards.
3. Annual fee.
4. Broker's commissions.
5. Margin loan rates.
6. Whether earnings are paid in cash directly to the investor or are automatically deposited in a money market fund.
7. How often earnings are paid or deposited in a money market fund.
8. What the money market fund invests in; for example, some invest only in government securities.

Investing in mutual funds

The emphasis in previous pages has been on your personal planning and execution of an investment program. If you feel you lack the time, ability, or temperament for such a program, you might consider mutual funds. Instead of investing directly in securities, you invest in a fund which manages a portfolio of securities. Mutual funds also enable an investor to diversify holdings and a small investor to enter the market with little capital.

Mutual funds pool the capital of many individuals to purchase stocks and bonds or specialized investments, such as gold funds, convertible bonds, real estate ventures, or foreign companies. Money market funds and tax-exempt municipal bond funds also come under the heading of mutual funds.

Mutual funds are professionally managed so the individual investor does not have to select stocks or plan when to buy and sell. However, despite experienced management, some funds do not succeed. You should research a fund's past performance and use caution before investing.

Mutual funds vary widely in objectives and in return to investors. Are you looking for long-term gain or current income? You will want to choose a fund in line with your investment goals.

There are two basic types of mutual funds: closed end and open end. Closed-end funds issue a specific number of shares when formed and, since they do not intend to issue more, are "closed end." Shares are traded on the stock exchange or over the counter, and in buying or selling you use a broker as you do in common stock transactions.

An open-end company is called "open end" because its capitalization is unlimited. Such companies create and sell shares whenever you want them, and buy them back and retire the shares whenever you want to cash in your chips. In other words, you join by turning over your funds to the company and getting newly created shares which represent your pro rata share of the entire fund.

Today the term "mutual fund" generally applies to open-end companies, and the discussion in this chapter deals primarily with open-end funds. Open-end mutual funds vary in the type of investment and element of risk. The prospectus of each fund will identify its objective. Here are some types of open-end funds available:

Growth funds. The objective of these funds is to achieve growth in the value of shares, which eventually leads to growth in capital. Dividend return tends to be low because these funds want to attract the long-term investor who looks for capital appreciation. Growth fund assets are usually invested in common stock up to about 90%. There are a number of types of growth funds, some of which are riskier than others.

Income funds. Investments here are primarily in high-yield securities, mainly corporate stocks and bonds. There are differences within this category, as some income funds will take risks in order to give shareholders a higher yield. Conservative investors, particularly older individuals looking for income, shun these funds.

Growth and income funds. Combining investments in stocks and bonds, these funds endeavor to give shareholders both high dividends and growth.

Because so many mutual funds are in "families," i.e., a group of funds managed by one company, shareholders in one type of fund within the family can switch to other types easily; also, it is no longer difficult to switch to a competing fund. A modest fee may be charged for group transfers or there may be no charge.

Most mutual funds pay quarterly dividends; some pay semi-annually. The amounts will vary depending on fund earnings. The fund receives a return on its investments, and members' shares are distributed in proportion to holdings after management fees and operating expenses are deducted. In addition, capital gains distributions resulting from profitable security sales by the fund may be made to shareholders. If desired, funds reinvest shareholders' dividends and capital gains and thus increase the investment. Mutual fund shares can be redeemed at any time.

Buying mutual funds

Open-end mutual funds are bought either through brokerage offices or selling organizations in the case of "load" funds, and directly from the fund in the case of "no-loads." The terms refer to sales charges or the lack of them, as explained below.

If you refer to the mutual fund listing in the financial pages of the *Wall Street Journal,* for example, you will find a listing with such entries as:

	NAV	Offer Price	NAV chg.
Fund X	19.84	N.L.	+.10
Fund Y	11.79	12.64	+.03

"NAV" stands for net asset value per share. "NAV Chg." indicates the change from the previous day. The offering price includes net asset value plus maximum sales charge, if any. An entry listed "N.L." (no load) means that there is no sales charge. An increasing number of funds are no-loads. At one time, load funds (those with sales charges) were represented as superior in management to no-loads, but the record of no-loads in recent years indicates that this is not necessarily so. In choosing a fund, decide on the type of fund you want and check its record. Do not make your decision based on charges or the lack of them. Obviously, many investors prefer to avoid sales charges if they can find a fund to their liking; this explains the number of funds now available in the no-load category. You will note from the listings that many fund families will offer both types.

While no-loads are generally handled directly by mail, some brokerage houses may also handle them.

You can buy mutual funds by making a large single investment or you can invest fixed amounts over a period. A minimum investment will be required in any case. It should be noted that both load and no-load funds charge an annual management fee. Before you invest, look for other charges such as redemption fees. The fund's prospectus will alert you. Ask yourself if investing in funds where charges run high is justified in terms of their record.

An open-end fund will redeem your shares at your request for the net asset value of the fund, which approximates the market value of all the securities owned by the fund divided by the number of shares. As market prices vary each day, the net asset value fluctuates.

Sources of information on mutual funds

Mutual fund data are readily available. The public information center for the industry is the Investment Company Institute, 1775 K Street, NW, Washington, DC 20006. Many no-load funds are represented by the No-Load Mutual Fund Association, Valley Forge, PA 19481.

Also seek out the *Mutual Fund Directory,* published by the Investment Dealers Digest, 150 Broadway, New York, NY 10038. Weisenberger Financial Services, c/o Warren, Garham & Lamont, 210 South St., Boston, MA 02111, publishes *Panorama,* an annual mini-prospectus on the funds and other funds information. *Forbes* magazine, 60 Fifth Avenue, New York, NY 10011, publishes a special annual issue on mutual funds.

Study the market quotations on mutual funds which are carried daily in many newspapers. While the history of many funds has generally been good, like other investments they have slipped in bear markets.

The records of closed-end companies are found in all the standard manuals. Most of them are traded on the stock exchanges and their day-to-day price fluctuations are easily followed in publications such as the *Wall Street Journal,* the *New York Times,* other city newspapers, and *Barron's.* If material is unavailable at a library, check stockbrokers' offices.

Study the market quotations on mutual funds which are carried daily in many newspapers. While the history of many funds has generally been good, like other investments they have slipped in bear markets. The newcomer to mutual fund investment has no guarantee that funds which have consistently made a good showing will do so in the future.

The funds themselves will be happy to mail you their literature. Through your reading and inquiries, you can increase your understanding of mutual funds. If you decide to buy, you will do so from an informed background.

Investment clubs

Another way of investing with a group, but on a much smaller scale, is an investment club which provides an inexpensive way to invest in the stock market. These clubs are currently enjoying a revival; many had disbanded after the stock market slump of 1973–1974.

. . . an investment club . . . provides an inexpensive way to invest in the stock market.

Investment clubs are usually small, often 15–20 people who pool their funds to buy a portfolio of stocks by investing a set amount monthly, which can be as little as $25 per person. Unlike mutual funds, investment clubs require the active involvement of the members who must meet regularly to manage their portfolio and agree on investment policy.

The National Association of Investment Clubs (NAIC) is an organization which helps to form new clubs. It advises a basic investment strategy: invest in growth companies (i.e., companies whose earnings and dividends outperform the industry average); invest regularly, whether the market looks good or bad; and reinvest earnings for compounding.

Although the amounts involved in investment clubs are generally low, many have good growth rates. Each club can decide its own investment policy. Some are more speculative than others; some put money in investments other than stocks. The NAIC suggests that investment clubs try for a 15% annual growth rate in their portfolios.

It is easier to start a new investment club than to join an ongoing one. To form a club, choose people who have investment ideas similar to your own; many new clubs dissolve when members disagree on investment strategy. Most clubs use discount brokers because their fees are lower than regular brokers; but remember that discount brokers do not generally give investment advice. For tax advice and regular accounting, consult professionals. Even if you do not wish to start a new club, you can still join the NAIC. For information, write to the NAIC, 1515 East Eleven Mile Road, Royal Oak, MI 48067.

Chapter 4

USING CREDIT

BUYING on credit has become an integral part of personal finances for most Americans. Credit is so readily available that it can be either a blessing or a curse, depending on how it is used. As long as you recognize that credit represents a debt you have to pay and are prepared through careful financial planning to pay within the stated time, you can profit from the convenience that buying on credit offers.

Your credit rating and credit bureaus

To obtain credit from a store, bank, or other financial institution, you must be a good risk. Thus your credit standing is a major asset to protect. You build up a credit history over the years.

. . . your credit standing is a major asset to protect.

When you apply for credit, your application is generally referred to a credit bureau, a company whose sole business it is to check credit references. Your credit record is available to creditors across the country.

If your application is turned down, do not consider your case closed. It is your right to know why you have been denied credit. The company denying you credit must tell you which credit bureau supplied the data. You may obtain a copy of your credit history at no charge if you request it within 30 days after credit has been denied. Inaccurate data must be corrected and a new report furnished to creditors. If you do not agree with the report after reinvestigation, you may submit your own written statement offering an explanation about the information to which you object. Your statement will remain with your credit record.

Note that negative credit information, such as the failure to pay a bill, should be removed from your record after seven years; judgments and lawsuits against you may generally remain on file for only ten years, and bankruptcies must be removed after ten years.

Even if your credit rating remains unchallenged, you are permitted to review your file. A nominal fee may be charged. You may inquire about your rights under the law by writing to the Bureau of Consumer Protection, Federal Trade Commission, Washington, DC 20580.

Establishing credit

Even if you do not feel the need to apply for a credit card or bank loan now, it may be wise to start establishing a good credit record. At some later time you may wish to borrow a substantial amount of money, say, for a home mortgage, and creditworthiness will be mandatory.

To obtain credit, you must first have an income. Second, establish checking and savings accounts in your own name to give you financial references. The next step is proving that you pay bills on time. If you are repaying an education loan, make your payments on time since that will appear on your credit record. Paying telephone and utility bills promptly is also a good indication of creditworthiness.

For first-time credit, you may apply for a department store credit card, which is generally easier to obtain than a bank card or a travel and entertainment card or a bank loan. If you are a graduating college senior who has accepted a job that pays at least $10,000 a year, you may request a special student credit card application from American Express.

For first-time credit, you may apply for a department store credit card, which is generally easier to obtain than a bank card or a travel and entertainment card or a bank loan.

When you apply for credit, the department store, bank, or finance company will require that you fill out a form listing your financial resources. You will be asked for your employer's name, your salary and other income, and details about home mortgages or rent, bank accounts, and your other credit cards. Make sure that your answers to those questions will stand up to investigation. If you fail to give full or truthful information, you will damage your credit record.

Consumer protection laws

The Truth in Lending Act was created to let consumers know the true costs of using credit. Your creditors must disclose the annual interest rate you will be paying. If your charge account is revolving, you must also be told the monthly interest rate and the minimum monthly payment. In addition, the company must inform you of the cash price of your purchase and the deferred payment price (except for a mortgage). Creditors must disclose the amount of down payment required, whether there is any penalty for prepayment and how the unearned part of the finance charge is calculated, and what penalty will be imposed if you pay late or default. On installment plans and loans, you must be told the number of payments, the amount of each, the due dates or period of payments, and whether there is a balloon payment, i.e., a final payment which is much higher than earlier payments.

The Equal Credit Opportunity Act prohibits creditors from discriminating against applicants on the basis of sex, marital status, race, color, religion, national origin, age, or even on the basis of receipt of public assistance.

Women, especially single and divorced women, have traditionally been discriminated against when seeking credit. But the law now limits the basis creditors may use to grant or deny credit to applicants. If you are married, your own income, whether from full or part-time work, must be considered. A divorced woman does not have to state that she receives alimony unless she wants to show that income to increase her chances of being a good credit risk. A creditor may not ask a woman about the financial status of her husband or ex-husband unless she relies on his income or alimony, or if he will use the account or be liable for it. However, if you live in a community property state, your husband's finances can be questioned. If your marital status changes, you may not be denied credit unless you are no longer able to make payments. Generally, women, whether married or single, should establish credit in their own names.

A creditor may not ask questions about childbearing plans or birth control practices. But if you have children, a creditor may ask about them to estimate your expenses.

In recent years, the number of credit complaints from women has decreased. However, if you think you have been discriminated against in a credit application, you should contact the Federal Trade Commission or a local government office dealing with discrimination problems.

Credit cards

Bank cards. Credit cards, such as MasterCard and VISA, are perhaps the best known and most widely accepted forms of credit. Some banks offer the cards free to customers; others charge an annual fee, typically $12 to $15, and may also charge a small fee for each transaction.

You do not incur any interest charges if you pay your bill in full by the date specified on your monthly bill. If you do not pay in full, interest will begin to accrue on the outstanding balance *plus* any new purchases. There are usually two interest rates: one that applies to balances of less than $500 and a slightly lower one that applies to balances of $500 or more. Your bill will give a breakdown of interest charges.

Travel and entertainment cards. The most familiar of these cards are American Express and Diner's Club. There is an annual membership fee of $35, $40 or more for travel and entertainment cards. Cardholders are expected to pay each bill in full by the payment date; partial payment is usually not allowed. Travel and entertainment card organizations offer added privileges such as travel accident insurance, worldwide access to cash, and check-guaranteeing services at better restaurants, theaters, stores, and luxury hotels.

Store or company cards. Many businesses, from department stores to oil companies, issue their own cards for purchasing their own goods and services. Credit terms vary; read carefully the accompanying disclosure statement that comes with each charge card.

Many businesses that issue their own cards also accept bank cards.

Debt problems

Because credit cards are so easy to use, you must discipline yourself so that your total debt does not get out of hand. Keep track of how much you are charging, where, and when. Do not allow your charges to exceed what you can afford to pay back each month.

Also ask yourself: Is it really necessary to delay payments? Could you pay for the item immediately? Consider that the cost of buying on credit may be as much as 21% a year or higher. If you buy $4,000 worth of merchandise on time, you will pay approximately $800 in finance charges. The amount you save by paying cash could be used for other purposes.

As a rule of thumb, if 10% or less of your take-home pay is spent to reduce your debt (exclusive of mortgage or rent), you are not overextended.

If you are charging merchandise, gasoline, services, entertainment, or travel and do not have the income to cover payments, put yourself on a strictly cash basis until your financial affairs are under control.

As a rule of thumb, if 10% or less of your take-home pay is

spent to reduce your debt (exclusive of mortgage or rent), you are not overextended. If 15% of pay is used to make monthly payments on credit accounts, be cautious about incurring any new charges. If you spend 20% of your pay on monthly charge accounts and loans, you are at a dangerous level and should stop incurring new debt until some accounts are paid off.

If your credit payments have gotten out of hand, meet with your creditors and explain your situation. They may be willing to work out a regular plan of lower payments each month, perhaps taken directly from your paycheck. If creditors know that a debtor is ready to handle repayment systematically, they are more likely to sit down and help work out a repayment schedule.

If debts are too heavy and it is impossible to handle repayments from income, there may be no alternative but to obtain a loan to consolidate all the debts. You use one loan to pay off the previous small debts but pay for the service in added interest charges.

If too much debt is a recurring burden, you may benefit from financial counseling. You can contact the Consumer Credit Counseling Service in your area or, for the name of a counseling center near you, you can write to the National Foundation for Consumer Credit, 8701 Georgia Ave., Silver Springs, MD 20910. This organization is supported by banks, retailers, and unions, and provides free budgeting aid. There may be a small charge for debt-repayment services. Fees are generally higher at private credit counseling services. Also, some credit unions and banks offer financial counseling to members and customers.

Payment of credit accounts

One problem with the payment of some credit accounts is the imposition of service charges on amounts you have already paid. Sometimes the trouble arises because your payment has not reached the company's accounting department before the next billing period. But some stores deliberately use this type of billing, especially on revolving charge accounts. Under this "previous balance" system, partial payments are not deducted when interest is computed. If the store used the "adjusted balance" system, taking payments and credits into consideration before computing interest, you would pay less interest.

Some states have rules against the use of the previous balance system, but allow companies to use the "average daily balance" to compute bills. Under this plan, you get credit for your payments, but are charged interest in proportion to the time your balance was not reduced by the payment.

If you have a complaint about a store's billing practices and can get no redress, make your complaint known. Some local newspapers and radio stations handle consumer grievances. You can also write to the Better Business Bureau, Federal Trade Commission, or your state attorney-general.

Handling disputed charge account bills

The creditor must mail your bill at least 14 days before payment is due. If you question a charge or the amount of your bill, you should call the telephone number supplied on the bill. Some problems can be handled promptly by phone.

If your question is not answered properly by phone, you should pay only the undisputed portion of the bill and write a letter to the company. The creditor must answer your letter within 30 days and your complaint must be resolved within 90 days. An address for inquiries and complaints must be given on the bill. Moreover, open-end creditors must identify each transaction on the monthly statement.

No collection letters may be sent to you while your bill is in dispute, and the creditor must inform the credit reporting agency so that no unfavorable credit information is issued on an unresolved matter. When the dispute is settled, the credit bureau is informed. If a creditor fails to comply with the requirements of the law, the penalty is the amount of the bill in dispute, up to $50, even if the bill was not in error.

A credit cardholder can withhold payment for defective merchandise worth over $50 and purchased within 100 miles of his home and need not be held liable for the entire amount owed.

Guarding against misuse of your credit card

Credit card abuse and theft is rampant. To protect yourself against the misuse of your credit card, make sure that each sales slip is accurate when purchases are written up. If errors require a new sales slip, see to it that the old one is destroyed.

If you lose your credit card, you are liable for up to $50 for unauthorized use of your card. However, as the $50 is on a per-card basis, your liability may be sizable if you lose several credit cards. You can limit your liability to zero if you report each card loss prior to any unauthorized use. Keep a list of the telephone numbers to call in case of theft or loss, along with your credit card account numbers. Follow up each call with a letter and keep a copy. If you lose a bank or travel and entertainment card, you may have to pay the annual membership fee again to have it replaced.

If, after reporting the loss of your credit cards, you find they were only misplaced, notify the companies immediately. Your card numbers will have been put on a stolen card list and using them could place you in an embarrassing situation.

Credit card insurance coverage may be bought separately or, in some cases, added to personal policies such as homeowners' or casualty policies. You may at the same time acquire other benefits, such as insurance against loss on altered checks, but you may also have to prove that you handled your cards with due care and reported loss immediately. This type of insurance is generally not advised.

Bank credit plans

Bank credit plans are usually known as convenience credit or overdraft checking accounts; details vary, but the plan terms are basically the same.

You are, in effect, writing a loan to yourself each time you use the convenience credit account.

With a convenience credit account, you have a credit line of up to, say, $5,000 and make use of the credit whenever you write a special check on that account. You pay a monthly interest charge currently about 20%, on the amount of credit actually used, and a fee is usually charged for the checks. As you repay the amount borrowed plus interest, you establish the right to use your credit account again. You are, in effect, writing a loan to yourself each time you use the convenience credit account.

Under an overdraft system, no special checks are required. A borrower of good standing can obtain a credit reserve of between $400 and $5,000 and may write checks for more than is currently on deposit in a regular checking account. Repayment each month is subject to a minimum amount, and more checks can be written, thereby adding to the debt. The annual rate of interest has been as high as 20%. More than one type of repayment plan is available. You can have overdraft checking for years and never use the credit feature, but it is available if you need it. If you do use it, make sure that deposits to your checking account go toward paying off the overdraft first. Some bank customers have found deposits building in the checking account while interest charges add up on unpaid overdraft balances.

Bank debit cards

When you use a credit card, you are using someone else's money to pay your obligations, but with a debit card (also called a cash card) you are using your own funds. There are two kinds of debit cards. One allows you access to your funds

---

Debit card owners save money by not having to pay interest charges; however, they do not have the benefit of credit card "float."

---

at electronic machines after banking hours. The other is similar to a credit card; it is used to pay for purchases and services. Each use of the card automatically deducts the amount spent from your account. Debit card owners save money by not having to pay interest charges; however, they do not have the benefit of credit card "float," i.e., using the bank's money to make purchases and keeping their money in an interest bearing account until the bill arrives. Both VISA and Master-Card offer debit cards, but they are not yet widely used.

Despite the attraction of convenient access to your money, there are some problems in owning a debit card for use at electronic machines. In case of loss, you can limit your liability for unauthorized use of your card to $50 if you notify your bank within two business days of loss. If you report the loss between the second and 60th day, you may be liable for up to $500 of unauthorized use. If you fail to notify the bank after 60 days, you are without recourse and your entire account could be wiped out.

In addition to incurring costs for unauthorized use of your cards, your new card may be intercepted and used without your being aware of it. Always arrange to pick up a new card in person. Store your personal identification number in a safe place and do not keep a copy of it in your wallet or purse. It is important to commit this number to memory.

Finally, the area around an electronic cash machine is an obvious target for thieves and muggers. If you are accosted after leaving the machine with cash, you must shoulder the loss without recourse to the bank.

Installment buying

If you are considering an installment sale purchase, here are some points to weigh:

Your ability to make a substantial down payment. A large initial payment will reduce the amount and spread of payments, as well as the finance charges you will pay. If you do not have the means to make a substantial down payment, think twice about whether you should be undertaking the installment payments.

What will your other commitments be during the period you will be paying on time? Have you left yourself a cash margin for emergencies? It is not possible to safeguard against all eventualities, but a heavy load assumed for a long period drives many families into debt from which they cannot easily escape.

The repayment period. Interest charges mount up during the spread-out paying period. Pay off your debt as quickly as you can. The shorter the period of repayment, the lower the overall cost. And, too, consider the length of time the item purchased will be useful to you; do not commit yourself to a term of repayment that exceeds the usefulness of the purchase.

For example, do not pay off a car over four years that you expect to keep only three years.

Under the law, before you sign any installment contract, you must be told:

1. The cash price of your purchase and the deferred payment price.
2. The amount of the down payment, or that none is required.
3. The number of payments to be made, the amount of each, and the due dates of payments.
4. The amount of the finance charge expressed as an annual percentage rate.
5. The amount of penalty, if any, for prepayment of your debt and how the unearned part of the finance charge is calculated; what penalty would be imposed if you are late with your payments, or if you default entirely. Take note that even if the creditor is entitled to repossess the goods, it may not relieve you of your obligation to pay.

In addition, you must receive a copy of the installment contract and a notice of cancellation. Before signing anything, however, make sure all the blank spaces have been filled in. Keep the copy of the contract in a safe place.

The best protection any consumer can have is to be cautious when signing a contract; check all its points and consider the legal commitments.

Whether a contract is offered to you by a ready-money lender, by a store where you are to pay on the installment plan, or by a door-to-door salesman, you should know that the contract is likely to be sold to a third party, such as a bank or sales finance company. If you pay on time, there is no trouble; but if you do not, the buyer of the contract has the legal rights set out in the contract. He may repossess the property, take over any security, have your wages garnisheed, or have a wage assignment made. The contract may hold you liable for costs and the creditor's attorney's fees if you are taken to court. And finally, the credit bureau will be notified, and this will affect your ability to get credit in the future.

Federal and state laws, as well as various consumer groups, are gradually coming to the aid of bewildered consumers who have failed to fulfill contracts that they have signed. In some cases the contract has not set out the debtor's rights as required by law; often the debtor did not fully understand the contract; frequently the penalty is excessive, as where the goods are repossessed and the debtor is still liable to pay for them. Nevertheless, the weight of the law is still with the creditor. The best protection any consumer can have is to be cautious when signing a contract; check all its points and consider the legal commitments.

Familiarize yourself with the laws in your state concerning consumer recourse in the event of faulty merchandise. If you are buying on installments and the merchandise proves defective, you may only have a limited time in which to lodge a complaint. Once that time is passed, you have no redress; you still owe payments on a faulty or useless item.

If you need a loan

If you find that you need a loan to purchase a house, a business, a car, to finance education, to consolidate your debts, or to meet an emergency, shop around. Terms and interest rates vary. Similarly, when money for loans is tight, you may not be able to borrow at the first bank or institution you turn to, but do not give up. If your credit rating is good, you should be able to locate a source of funds.

If, through no fault of your own, you do not have an established credit rating, obtaining a loan may be difficult. Then you may need a person who has the required financial standing, such as a friend or relative, to cosign a note at a bank or finance company. Your comaker, who believes in your integrity and ability to repay, takes equal responsibility for settling with the lender if you default.

If, on the other hand, you are asked to cosign a loan, do so only if the borrower is a relative or friend you know well and in whom you have complete confidence. Be confident of your ability to pay in the event you are called upon to do so. Even a cosigner's credit rating may be in jeopardy if the borrower defaults.

Borrowing on your life insurance policy

Your life insurance policy may make a loan available to you at exceptionally low interest rates, although insurance loans at low rates may be on the way out. The insurance industry is advocating interest rates comparable to market rates by abolishing state-imposed interest ceilings.

If you borrow on your policy, be aware that your loan reduces your family's protection in the event of your death.

You can borrow most of your policy's cash value. Reread your policy; cash value and loan rates will be stated. Write your company, giving your policy number, and state how much you want. Usually, a check will be sent within a few days, no questions asked, and you can repay on a system convenient to you.

If you borrow on your policy, be aware that your loan reduces your family's protection in the event of your death. The very lack of pressure to repay an insurance loan is not in its favor on a long-term basis. By constantly postponing full discharge of the loan, you heighten the risk of being underinsured. You also lack that cushion of financial assurance your insurance policy offers should you have to meet an even greater emergency in the future.

Borrowing from your savings institution

When the need for a loan arises, the person who saves regularly at a bank or savings and loan association has an advantage. An individual who has a passbook savings account can do without a loan, and instead draw on his or her account for the needed funds; the only cost is the interest lost while the money is gone.

If you have a savings account but do not wish to deplete your funds, consider a loan against the account. The savings institution will advance you the sum you need at a comparatively reasonable rate (for example, 2% above the savings account rate) and, at the same time, you do not lose the interest accumulating in your savings account. All the time you are repaying your loan, your savings account continues to earn interest. The cost of the loan is essentially the difference between the interest rate charged and the rate earned on your account.

The proliferation of bank credit cards has had an impact on loans. Where installment loans were once touted, today customers are encouraged to use their bank credit cards for small loans, say, up to $2,000. This type of loan is called a cash advance. You pay the interest rates permitted in your state. And you may pay interest on interest. This occurs if you fail to pay your monthly balance so that you incur interest on it. Next month that interest is added to the balance you owe, and interest is figured on the total amount, not only on your debt.

If you investigate loan terms at banks and thrifts, you will find that they vary even within the same area. Some institutions will not offer loans in a specific category, e.g., autos, consumer goods, or personal; some offer loans at the same interest rate in all three categories. The cheapest loans are usually those secured by collateral, or savings account loans from your thrift institution. However, if you are a member of a credit union, you may be able to obtain an even lower rate on loans.

The proliferation of bank credit cards has had an impact on loans. Where installment loans were once touted, today customers are encouraged to use their bank credit cards for small loans, say, up to $2000.

If you put up stocks and bonds as collateral at a commercial bank, the bank holds your stocks and you sign a "time note." This note may become due before you are ready to repay, but if your securities still have high market value, your note can probably be renewed. When you repay the loan, your securities are returned to you.

Be alert to several factors when considering this type of loan. You will receive less than the current market value of your securities as a loan. That is the bank's way of protecting itself against the possible decline in your securities' value. You will not be asked to put up additional security unless the stock drops to below the actual amount of the loan.

If you cannot pay the loan but the value of your stock has increased, the bank will sell all or part of your stock. It collects only the debt; you may collect some profit.

Your pledged stocks and bonds still pay you the usual dividends, which helps to offset the cost of your loan.

Use small loan companies as a last alternative

Most states require small loan companies to be licensed. In this way, you can be satisfied that they are reputable and operating within the law.

Typically, loan companies keep usual business hours. Processing your loan application may be faster and less involved. But in return for speed and lack of intensive questioning, you pay their high interest rates. If funds are borrowed for a short time, say six months, make sure you determine the annual interest rate. This is explained later in this chapter.

The small loan company can assist the person without a credit background to consolidate debts and thereby to improve his future standing. Some will provide competent budgeting and counseling services which are of real benefit to people who cannot see their way through a difficult financial situation.

In general, go to the small loan company only if you cannot get a loan from a lower rate source. If you do so, check on the company first through the local Better Business Bureau.

Credit costs and true rate of interest

If you decide to buy on credit or to borrow money, you will want to know how much it is costing you to use the lender's money—both in terms of dollars and rate of interest. Then you can compare the varying prices of credit and buy or borrow at the lowest cost. Or you might find that you cannot afford to use credit—the price may be beyond your means.

The law requires the lender to disclose the annual percentage rate of interest and other pertinent information. However, some companies still fail to comply with the law and generally take advantage of customer confusion and ignorance. Below is a discussion on figuring interest rates. By substituting your own figures in our examples, you will be able to check on the costs of a loan or installment purchase.

Types of loans and ways of stating interest

When you "buy now, pay later," "charge it," "buy on time," "use a payment plan," and whenever you take out a loan, you are using someone else's money—and paying for the use of it. How much it costs depends on the terms of the credit agreement.

Simple interest. A loan at simple interest at 12% a year means that you pay 12¢ a year for each dollar you borrow. If you borrow $100 at 12% for a full year and do not have to pay monthly installments, you would have the full use of the money until the end of the year. At the end of the year, you would repay $112. You would then be paying a true annual interest of 12%. If you repaid the loan in six months, the interest would be half, or $6. The 12% simple interest comes to 1% a month.

Add-on loan. With an add-on loan, the interest charge is added to your loan or purchase. On a 15% per $100 loan for a year you have to repay $115. If you make monthly repayments, you do not have the full use of the money for the entire year. Month by month you have less, but you are still paying on $100 at 15% a year. If you repay the $100 plus 15% interest in 12 monthly installments of $9.58 each for a total of $115, your true annual interest is 27.7%, almost double what you thought you were paying. If your repayments are scheduled over 18 months, you would be repaying $123 (15% per year for 1½ years). Your monthly payments would be lower, $6.83 per month; your true rate of interest would be higher, 29.1%.

Discount loan. On a discounted loan, the bank discounts or deducts the interest in advance. On a one-year $100 discounted loan at 12% interest, you actually receive only $88; you have to repay $100. Each monthly installment comes to $8.33. Your true annual interest is 25.1%.

The discount method actually works out to a higher rate of interest than the add-on loan because the same $12 of interest is a larger share of $88 than it is of $100. Roughly, true annual interest on a discounted loan paid back in monthly installments over a year is about double the rate stated.

Under the law, the true annual interest must be disclosed to you. But if you wish to determine the figure for yourself, you can do so by applying the following formula:

$$\text{TRUE ANNUAL INTEREST} = \frac{\left(\begin{array}{c}2 \times \text{number of}\\ \text{installments in year}\end{array}\right) \times \$ \text{ cost of loan}}{\left(\begin{array}{c}\text{amount of loan}\\ \text{actually received}\end{array}\right) \times \left(\begin{array}{c}\text{total number of}\\ \text{installments} + 1\end{array}\right)}$$

For example, you take out a loan of $1,000, quoted at 6% per $100 discounted, to be repaid monthly over two years. This means you receive only $880; $120 is the cost of the loan. You figure the true annual interest by applying the above formula as follows:

$$\text{TRUE ANNUAL INTEREST} = \frac{2 \times 12 \times \$120}{\$880 \times (24 + 1)} = 13.1$$

This works out to 13.1% true annual interest.

Or say you plan to purchase a washing machine costing $300. The dealer offers you $25 for your old washer as a trade-in and quotes you a price of $36 to cover carrying charges to finance the new purchase over an 18-month period. You can check the true annual rate of interest you would be paying by applying the formula:

$$\text{TRUE ANNUAL INTEREST} = \frac{2 \times 12 \times \$36}{\$275 \times (18 + 1)} = 16.5$$

The finance charges on the washing machine would come to 16.5% in true annual interest.

As a result of law changes requiring disclosure of annual interest rates, discount loans are increasingly less popular and are being displaced by add-on loans.

Unpaid balance—monthly interest. Credit unions and small loan companies, as well as retail merchants and banks on certain types of charge plans, quote charges as a percentage of the balance unpaid each month. The true annual interest rate must be disclosed. You may check for yourself by multiplying the monthly interest by 12.

MONTHLY RATE	TRUE ANNUAL RATE
¾ of 1%	9%
⅚ of 1%	10%
1%	12%
1¼%	15%
1½%	18%
1¾%	21%
2%	24%
2¼%	27%
2½%	30%
2¾%	33%
3%	36%

As you repay the amount borrowed, the size of the loan decreases. For example, say your unpaid balance is $120 and is repayable in 12 monthly installments at 1% per month. Figure your interest charge on the unpaid balance at the end of the month as follows:

Divide $120 by 12 to find the amount of principal you must repay each month:

$$\$120 \div 12 = \$10$$

Determine the 1%-a-month interest charge payable on $120, your unpaid balance at the end of the first month:

$$\$120 \times 1\% = \$1.20$$

Your first payment is $11.20; $10 principal and $1.20 interest. Subtract your monthly principal payment from the balance:

$$\$120 - \$10 = \$110$$

The second month you repay $10 of principal and 1% interest on your remaining balance of $110 or $1.10 so your payment is $11.10.

Figure your payments of principal and interest this way each month. Remember, your principal payment remains the same; the interest charge decreases as your unpaid balance is reduced. Your final payment on the loan will be $10.10.

This $120, 1%-a-month loan actually costs 12% per year in interest; in dollars it costs $7.80.

Bankruptcy

Some people run so far into debt that bankruptcy seems to be the only way out. Consider bankruptcy as a final alternative, one you should work to avoid. Though some advertisements sell bankruptcy as an easy way out of debt problems, the debtor pays a heavy price financially and emotionally.

A study financed by an organization of creditors showed that 29% of persons who filed for bankruptcy under Chapter 7 of the new act could have paid all their debts over five years and that 75% of them held full-time jobs.

The number of personal bankruptcies soared after the Bankruptcy Reform Act was passed in 1978. In the first year after the new act was passed, personal bankruptcies jumped 75%, according to Brimmer & Company, a financial consulting firm. Most people filing for bankruptcy were not struggling at the poverty level. In fact, Brimmer's report described the typical person filing for bankruptcy as well educated, aged 34 or younger, holding a stable job, living in the same residence for five or more years, and having a good payment record with creditors.

The new law—plus inflation and recession—have been blamed for the sharp increase in bankruptcies. Creditors are advocating stricter bankruptcy laws so changes may be forth-coming. A study financed by an organization of creditors showed that 29% of persons who filed for bankruptcy under Chapter 7 of the new act could have paid all their debts over five years and that 75% of them held full-time jobs.

Under current law, an individual may declare bankruptcy under Chapter 7 or Chapter 13. Chapter 7 is straight bank-ruptcy. The court arranges for a sale of your assets (though a number of assets are exempted under federal or state law). The proceeds of the sale are distributed to your creditors and the remaining debts are discharged.

Property used as collateral for a loan may be repossessed by the lender. This rule applies if the loan was given to buy the object that is collateral, e.g., an installment loan to buy a washing machine. If the loan was not used to buy the col-lateral and it is "sheltered property," the collateral cannot be seized. With the court's permission, you may agree to pay off some debts to keep certain items.

Under federal law, an individual may shelter (keep) the following when declaring bankruptcy:

Up to $7,500 equity in a home. If you do not own a home, this exemption can be used to shield other property.

Up to $1,200 interest in a car.

Clothes, household goods, appliances, books, up to a limit of $200 for each item.

Up to $500 worth of jewelry.

Up to $4,000 in cash value life insurance.

Up to $750 worth of books or tools of your trade.

Note: These amounts are doubled for married couples filing joint bankruptcy. However, these are federal limits; if a state disagrees with the amounts of federal exemptions, it may im-pose its own limits. Currently, 22 states do not follow the federal exemptions. In 18 states the debtor is allowed to choose between state and federal exemptions.

Some obligations are not eliminated under Chapter 7. These are taxes, alimony, child support, government student loans, damages for malicious injury, and debts incurred through fraudulent representation.

Under Chapter 13, you may keep your belongings by agreeing to a repayment plan. The court must approve the plan arranged between you and your creditors. The payments are usually made over a three-year period or less. You pay a set amount each month to the court which distributes the money to your creditors.

You may declare bankruptcy once every six years. Judges may refuse benefits to anyone who plans bankruptcy as a way to avoid paying bills.

Advantages:

1. When you file for bankruptcy, creditors may not start or continue any action against you. Your wages cannot be garnisheed, your home cannot be repossessed, etc.
2. After the court has ruled, no creditor can approach you to reaffirm a debt that has been discharged.

Disadvantages:

1. Though the stigma of bankruptcy has lessened, it still involves emotional pain and embarrassment. It can be a source of problems at work and at home.
2. Bankruptcy remains on your credit record for ten years. You may be unable to obtain credit for that period or only be allowed credit for items which can be readily repossessed.

Filing for bankruptcy is fairly inexpensive; in 1981 the filing fee was $60. You will probably want the help of a lawyer. Legal fees for bankruptcies run from $150 to $500.

Chapter 5

CONSUMER PROTECTION

AS a result of the consumer protection movement of the past decade, buyers have greater protection against fraud, faulty merchandise, and broken contracts. Nonetheless, consumer protection begins with you. Learn to shop wisely, especially when making a major purchase. Take your time; do not buy on impulse. Compare prices, ask about warranties, and buy from a reliable merchant who will stand by the product.

Warranties and guarantees

Most reputable firms offer written warranties or guarantees on their products. Not all firms stand by their warranties, but the majority do.

Read a warranty carefully to see what protection it offers. You can see a copy of the warranty in the store before you make a purchase. A warranty for a product that costs more than $15 must explain exactly what is or is not covered and what the manufacturer will do if the product fails. A warranty must also include the procedure to follow if the product needs repair. A warranty may be limited to the original purchaser.

105

When buying a product covered by a warranty, it is important to check out the service department that will handle repairs. Will you have to ship the product back to the manufacturer for service, or does the dealer have a repair shop? Or must you deal with a service agency? If you must return a product to a repair center, find out who pays shipping charges and whether you must pay for parts or labor. If your merchandise cannot be repaired, find out whether you are entitled to a cash refund or a replacement.

Service contracts

Many appliances and electrical items are now sold with service contracts. For an annual fee, service contracts cover the cost of repairs after the term of the warranty.

While service contracts offer a form of protection, they may not be worth the cost. A study funded by the National Science Foundation showed that service contracts were overpriced. While the currently high cost of repairs makes the contract look like a good deal, the expected cost of repairs over several years is lower than the cost of the contract for that period. However, even critics of service contracts admit that they can be useful to some consumers. Service contracts can provide peace of mind for the elderly and others who may not have the cash for sudden large repair bills. Other consumers who may benefit from service contracts are those who are hard on appliances or own an appliance that breaks down

Service contracts can provide peace of mind for the elderly and others who may not have the cash for sudden large repair bills.

frequently. For example, it may pay a family with eight children who buys a new clothes washer to invest in a service contract. The machine will get above-average use and will probably need repairs sooner than a washer purchased by a couple with no children.

If you consider buying a service contract, shop around via the Yellow Pages. Service contracts are sold by appliance manufacturers, dealers, and independent companies. Rates vary widely and so do the services and coverage promised in the contracts. In some areas, you may be able to get one contract which covers all or many of your appliances. Be sure you are not buying protection for something that is already covered by a warranty. Ask whether the contract is transferable to another owner in case you sell the appliance or whether the contract can be cancelled for a refund. Also find out whether there is a deductible amount you must pay.

Door-to-door sales

If you buy goods from a door-to-door salesperson, the law provides a three-day cooling-off period during which you may change your mind about the transaction. You may cancel a sales contract before midnight on the third business day after the date of the sale. The seller must furnish you with a notice in large, clear type telling you of this right to cancel, give you the form on which to write the cancellation, and supply his business name and address for its safe delivery.

If you have already taken delivery of the goods, you must arrange with the seller for their return in good condition; he is responsible for any shipping expenses. If you fail to return the goods as arranged, then the terms of the contract will stand and not be cancelled. On the other hand, if the seller receives your notice of cancellation and arranges to pick up the goods but does not do so within 20 days, you are under no further obligation to return them.

When you cancel, the seller must return to you any payments you made at the time you signed the contract. He has ten days in which to do so.

These rules apply to sales of more than $25 made anywhere other than the seller's normal place of business. It does not apply to sales made totally by phone or mail, or sales of real estate, insurance, securities, and work supplies.

Late delivery

Late delivery of household goods is a common problem. Try to have a delivery date written into your purchase contract. Also, arrange to make a down payment on the item when you buy and pay the balance on delivery. The seller then has more incentive to deliver on time.

Your city or state may have laws governing delivery dates. You can check out a store's reputation before shopping there. Call the local office of the Better Business Bureau and ask about complaints of late deliveries.

Home repair abuses

Home repair abuse and fraud are at the top of the list of consumer complaints. In 1980 they were also the most expensive ones. Since most homeowners do not have the technical knowledge or tools needed to make repairs on major appliances, homes, and property, they are forced to rely on outside help.

You can reduce the number of repairs or the chances of being cheated by taking the following steps:

1. Deal with local repair shops you know or those which have been recommended to you by others. Or call the manufacturer of an appliance for a recommendation of a repair shop. Do not hire a traveling group of workers; they may not finish the job or may do it improperly and will not be around later if their repairs are faulty.
2. Read instructions carefully before operating any new appliance.

A popular repair rip-off is waterproofing a basement by pumping clay or a chemical into the ground to seal the walls against leakage.

---

3. Before you buy, find out whether the item is covered by a warranty. Where are repairs done and who pays for them?
4. Before having repair work done, get a written estimate of the costs. Afterward, get a receipt and find out how long the repair shop guarantees the work.
5. Read all contracts carefully. Some home-repair contracts

may include a clause entitling the worker to foreclose on the house if you miss payments.

6. Beware of complicated-sounding repairs that promise too much or repair workers who volunteer to "examine" your home. In the latter case, they may find problems which do not exist, then offer you a "good deal" to repair them. A popular repair rip-off is waterproofing a basement by pumping clay or a chemical into the ground to seal the walls against leakage. According to the experts, this method usually does not work.

7. If repair workers or home-improvement companies must be licensed in your area, hire a worker or company that holds a current license.

8. For a home-improvement project, make sure the contract spells out all details, including exact materials to be used, when work will begin and end, prices, and a schedule of payments. Do not sign a contract which gives only a general description of work to be done.

9. When you are having work done on your home, try to pay a down payment, with the balance due after the work is completed.

Ordering goods by mail

Mail-order catalogs are enjoying renewed popularity. They offer the convenience of shopping at home without spending time and money traveling to stores. Sales by mail-order catalogs now account for 10% of all general merchandise sales and may increase as stores such as Sears begin to make their catalog accessible through cable TV.

While many mail-order businesses are reputable, some promise more than they can deliver. When buying by mail, you should be aware of your rights. The item you ordered must be shipped within the time stated in the advertisement, or within 30 days after the company receives payment. If the company cannot ship the item within 30 days, it must notify you and offer you either a refund or a later delivery date. (However, this rule does not apply to photo finishing, magazine subscriptions, or seed or plant orders. It also does not apply to book and record clubs which ship merchandise regularly unless you specifically instruct otherwise.)

If you do not respond when offered a choice of a later delivery date or a refund, the company may assume that you accept the later delivery date. If the company cannot deliver within another 30 days, it must again notify you. If you do not agree to accept delivery after the stated delay, the company

---

When ordering by mail, rely on the catalog description of the item, not its picture, to be sure it is really what you want.

---

must give you a refund. If you cancel a prepaid sale, the company must mail you a cash refund within seven business days or, on credit sales, remove the charge from your account within one billing cycle.

When ordering by mail, rely on the catalog description of the item, not its picture, to be sure it is really what you want. Also, be careful when filling out the order form as even a small mistake may delay your order. Pay by check, money order, or credit card, and hold on to your records until you receive the merchandise. Also, keep the catalog and note the date of your order.

If you have a problem with a mail-order company, first write to the company. If the problem is not resolved to your satisfaction, call the local consumer agency or the Better Business Bureau. Also ask your local postmaster how to register a complaint with the postal inspector-in-charge. Also, you can file complaints with the Mail Preference Service, Direct Mail/Marketing Association, 6 East 43rd Street, New York, NY 10017. This organization will also take your name off or add it to mailing lists if you request.

Making a move

Nearly one in five Americans moves every year, and many people rely on professional moving companies to handle much of the work involved. Moving can be expensive, but consumers should benefit from the increased competition in the moving industry caused by deregulation ordered by Congress in the

Household Goods Transportation Act of 1980. For example, some companies now offer discounts for paying in advance and to senior citizens.

A moving company may charge by space, by the hour, or by the weight of your goods. On interstate moves you are usually charged by weight, but you may find a company that charges by space instead.

With deregulation, more companies offer binding estimates, but if the estimate is more than the load's actual weight, you pay only for the actual weight. A company may protect itself by making high estimates. If you get a nonbinding estimate, you should check the weight of the truck at the weighing station before loading and return afterward to check the loaded weight. Some companies illegally add extra weight to their trucks to increase the bill.

You can buy insurance from moving companies to cover the value of your goods, but some companies will not insure jewelry, antiques, and other valuables.

Contact several companies for estimates and ask friends and relatives for recommendations of reliable movers; then check local consumer agencies for information on the companies you are considering. Also, obtain a copy of the Complaint and Performance Data on Household Goods Movers which is published every year by the Interstate Commerce Commission (ICC). The ICC also has a toll-free consumer hotline, 800/424-9312, to receive complaints and give information on moving. A number of moving companies belong to the American Movers Conference, an industry group that offers information on moving and an arbitration service to settle disputes between customers and movers.

You can buy insurance from moving companies to cover the value of your goods, but some companies will not insure jewelry, antiques, and other valuables. Minimum coverage of 60¢ per pound is free, but unless you request the minimum, you will get full-value liability for which you pay 50¢ per $100 of valuation. The cost will be approximately the load weight multiplied by $1.25. In the case of loss, depreciation is usually figured, but some movers no longer use this factor. Particularly valuable items should always be itemized on the bill of lading.

Another type of coverage is the broad trip policy. The moving company writes a policy to cover additional risks, according to your specifications. The cost is based on the distance of the move. An alternative to the broad-trip policy is a fine arts floater, which gives specialized coverage for specific items. Your insurance agent can advise you on the amount and cost.

There are other options for moving your goods. Air freight is more expensive but faster than moving by van. United Parcel Service and registered U.S. mail ship small items and may be good choices for transporting legal documents. You can have the contents of your safe deposit box sent directly to a bank in your new location. For valuable items, you may want to consider armored courier services, such as Wells Fargo, Brinks, or Purolater Armored, Inc. The charges of these services vary widely.

If you are driving to your new home, you can bring small items in your car or rent a trailer. The charge for the trailer will not be high, and you can insure your goods for the trip. A do-it-yourself move saves money, but requires hard work. When you rent a van, you will also be able to rent equipment, such as furniture pads and dollies. Even if you do not move the furniture yourself, you can save by packing your dishes, contents of closets, etc., instead of paying a moving company to pack them. You can buy special cartons for dishes and pick up used cardboard boxes free at local stores.

The peak season for moving is June through September, and moving companies charge their highest rates during this period. Also, avoid moving on holiday weekends.

Effective complaint letters

A product you purchase may be defective, a bill incorrect. You may wish to complain or you may be required to put your complaint in writing to get action. To help you resolve your problem by letter, here are some guidelines:

Despite your annoyance with the company, do not lose your temper in the letter. Its tone should be businesslike.

The letter should be typed so it looks professional and is easy to read.

Address the letter to the correct person—the store manager, department director, or company president. You can find the name and address by calling or looking in business directories, such as *Standard & Poor's Directory of Corporations, Directors and Executives.* For simple matters, a letter to the consumer service department may be sufficient.

The letter should be brief. State when and where you made the purchase, what happened, or what is defective. Then state what action you would like the company to take, such as sending a refund or a replacement. Include your name and address in the letter itself as well as on the envelope. Send copies of receipts, but never send the originals.

For simple matters, a letter to the consumer service department may be sufficient.

You can send a copy of the letter to consumer agencies and note the copies at the bottom of the letter. This notation may make your letter more impressive, although these agencies will only file your letter when they receive it. They will not act on your complaint unless you specifically request their aid.

If you do not receive a reply or the reply offers no acceptable solution, write another letter explaining your dissatisfaction. If the problem remains unresolved, seek the help of a consumer agency, such as the Better Business Bureau or a state consumer agency, or the consumer "help" column in a local newspaper. Keep copies of all correspondence and records of all telephone calls made in connection with your complaint.

Going to court

If your complaint cannot be settled, you may consider taking your dispute to court. However, unless damages are substantial, you may not want to incur costly legal fees. If you seek moderate redress, you may consider bringing your case to a Small Claims Court or court of similar jurisdiction, provided in many localities. You may sue in Small Claims Court if the amount of money involved is not more than the state's limit for the court, generally $1,000. You must sue for a dollar amount; you cannot sue for replacement goods or services. The company or person you are suing must have an office in the city where you are suing, or live or work there.

In most areas you do not need a lawyer, and the court fees are low. If you decide to sue, go to the court and explain your problem to the clerk, who will help you fill out the necessary forms. Your case will be heard a few weeks later by a judge or an arbitrator. If the company offers to settle out of court, get the terms in writing and notify the court.

Sometimes, a court victory is no guarantee of cash recovery. You may be forced to initiate further legal action to collect for your court award.

Directory of where to complain

When a store or manufacturer does not solve a problem to your satisfaction, you can turn to outside agencies for help. Check your telephone directory for the location and telephone number of your state or city Office of Consumer Affairs. Also, check a local office of the Better Business Bureau.

You may also contact the federal agencies listed below:

AGENCY	FOR PROBLEMS CONCERNING
Federal Trade Commission Pennsylvania Ave. at Sixth St. NW Washington, DC 20580 (tel. 202/523–3598)	Credit Warranties False advertising False labeling Fraud
Food and Drug Administration 2600 Fishers Lane Rockville, MD 20857 (tel. 301/443–4795)	Foods Cosmetics Medical products

AGENCY	FOR PROBLEMS CONCERNING
Housing and Credit Division Department of Justice Civil Rights Division Washington, DC 20530 (tel. toll free 800/424–8590)	Credit discrimination Housing discrimination
Interstate Commerce Commission Constitution Ave. and 12th St. NW Washington, DC 20423 (tel. toll free 800/424–9312)	Moving Interstate bus and train travel
Consumer Product Safety Commission 7315 Wisconsin Ave. NW Washington, DC 20016 (tel. toll free 800/638–8326)	Product safety
National Highway Traffic Safety Administration Department of Transportation 400 Seventh St. SW Washington, DC 20590 (tel. toll free 800/424–9393)	Auto safety Auto recall information
Office for Consumer Affairs U.S. Dept. of Housing and Urban Development 452 Seventh Ave. SW Washington, DC 20410 (tel. 202/634–4140)	Home builders
Division of Consumer Affairs Federal Reserve System 21st St. and Constitution Ave. NW Washington, DC 20551 (tel. 202/452–3204)	Banks that are members of the Federal Reserve system

AGENCY	FOR PROBLEMS CONCERNING
Office of the Secretary Federal Home Loan Bank Board 320 First St. NW Washington, DC 20552 (tel. toll free 800/424–5405)	Federally chartered savings and loan associations (for state- chartered S&Ls, contact your state's banking agency)
Office of the Administrator National Credit Union Ad- ministration 2025 M St. NW Washington, DC 20456 (tel. 202/357–1050)	Credit unions

Some industries have set up their own offices to handle consumer complaints. These include:

Major Appliances Consumer Action Panel 20 North Wacker Dr. Chicago, IL 60606	Appliances
AUTOCAP 8400 Westpark Dr. McLean, VA 22101	New car dealers
Furniture Industry Consumer Panel Box 951 High Point, NC 27261	Furniture
American Movers Conference Dispute Settlement Program 400 Army-Navy Dr. Arlington, VA 22202	Moving

Chapter 6

BUYING OR SELLING A CAR

IF you have not purchased a car within the last few years and are now in the market for one, you will soon experience the phenomenon called "sticker shock" when you enter a showroom and check the prices. It is not unusual to see a price tag of $10,000 on a model which only a few years

---

. . . buying a car today is a serious economic decision which requires thought, careful shopping, and patience.

---

ago cost $4,000. To add insult to injury, $4,000 will not even buy a new car now. If you check the used-car market, you will be jolted by cars selling for $2,000 or more which sold for $500 to $600 four or five years ago. Further, it is estimated that it now takes an average of 38% of a family's income to pay for a new car. Thus buying a car today is a serious economic decision which requires thought, careful shopping, and patience.

Pricing and buying a new car

The best way to get a good deal on a new car is to know what the car you want to buy *should* cost. Read newspaper advertisements for an idea of the price range; also look for stories in the business section of the newspaper about oversupplies of certain models. Dealers will often sell at lower prices to reduce swollen inventory. Also, dealers may be stuck with cars that were ordered by customers but not picked up. They may be anxious to sell unclaimed cars so you may get a good price, although the car may come with options you did not plan to buy. As with other major purchases, compare prices at different locations. You may be able to save as much as several hundred dollars at a big-volume dealer as opposed to a small dealership which must make a greater profit on each car sold.

You can find out the dealer's wholesale cost and suggested retail price by consulting car guides. Edmund Publications (515 Hempstead Turnpike, West Hempstead, NY 11552) publishes price guides for new American and European models as well as used cars. Davis Publications (380 Lexington Avenue, New York, NY 10017) publishes *Car/Puter's New Car Yearbook* and price guides for new and used cars. These books are sold at newsstands, bookstores, and by mail.

Three companies sell computerized printouts of new car costs. You fill out a form requesting the price for a specific model with the options you want and the printout tells you the factory price the dealer pays as well as the suggested sticker price. These companies can also arrange sales with local car dealers. The companies are:

Car/Puter
1603 Bushwick Ave.
Brooklyn, NY 11207

Nationwide Auto Brokers
17517 West Ten Mile Rd.
Southfield, MI 48075

Computerized Car Costs
Eleven Mile Lahser Station
Southfield, MI 48037

Knowing the dealer's cost gives you a ballpark figure with which to begin bargaining. You can expect to pay at least $100 to $200 over dealer's cost, but this figure usually goes higher for more expensive cars, foreign cars, and popular models.

Remember that options add to your cost. Find out what features are standard for the car. Pick only options that seem worth the price to you. Some models with an apparently higher sticker price may include features which you would have to order as options on a less expensive model. Take this into consideration when pricing different cars. Changes from the standard and options should be noted in the contract.

The advantage of buying a car from inventory is that you can test-drive it and see exactly what you are buying.

Another way to save money is to buy at the end of the month or in late summer or early fall when the new models are arriving and good deals are possible on the previous year's models. The middle of winter is also a good time to shop because sales are often slow. The best time of day to shop is an hour or two before closing when sales personnel may be eager to close a sale; but give yourself enough time to inspect the car and bargain for a price.

You may buy a car from a dealer's inventory; this is called a stock purchase. The advantage of buying a car from inventory is that you can test-drive it and see exactly what you are buying. Dealers like to sell from inventory because it shows an immediate profit for them. However, a dealer may not have the car you want in the right color and with the options you would choose.

Your other choice is to factory-order a car exactly as you want it. You may have to wait from four to six weeks or more for delivery. When your car arrives, make sure everything is as you ordered. If the dealer delays delivery and then tries to charge you more or includes expensive options you did not want, refuse the deal.

Some dealers will arrange a dealer trade for you, but many will not because of the extra work involved. In a dealer trade, your dealer trades a car from his inventory with another dealer who has the car you want in stock.

Bargaining. Dealers will not give you their best price if they think you are just window shopping. A serious customer will get their attention. After researching the price of the car, let the dealer know you have the funds to close the deal and will make a deal today if the price is right. If you want to arrange a trade-in, do not discuss it until the dealer gives you a new car price in writing.

Total cost. When you receive a price quote on a car, ask for the total cost, including all charges. On a new car, you will pay the following charges in addition to the sticker price:

> Dealer's prep charge—for the inspection the dealer
>   gives the car when it arrives from the factory.
> Freight charge—for shipping car from factory.
> Title and registration fees.
> Advertising costs (a share of the dealer's costs).
> Excise tax.
> Sales tax.

When you pick up your new car, you will also be charged for the gas in it.

Trade-in. If you want to trade in your old car, first get a firm price on a new car in writing. Then negotiate a price for your old car. You will probably get the best price from a dealer who sells that make. Beware of "high-balling," i.e., when a salesperson offers a high price for your car but the manager turns it down. You bargain with them and end up settling for a low price. (The opposite sales tactic is "low-balling," when a salesperson offers a low price on a new car to entice a buyer. When the buyer returns to close the deal, he or she is informed that the car has been sold, but the salesperson can get another one just like it—for more money.)

Deposit. Once you have given a deposit on a new car, it is considered binding on you and the seller. If you change your mind, you may not get your money back unless a refund of deposit clause was included in the contract or the seller is willing to make the refund. Your deposit will be refunded automatically if the sale is rejected by a dealer or dealer-obtained finance company.

Warranties. As an inducement for customers, more car manufacturers are offering better warranties. Warranties usually run for a stated number of years or thousands of miles, whichever comes first. A warranty protects you only to a certain extent, so read it carefully. Note that most warranties will not cover tires and normal maintenance charges, for example, changing spark plugs, and damages resulting from an accident or misuse. A manufacturer's warranty may be included with your purchase or you may have to pay for coverage. Further, where a manufacturer's free warranty is for a short term, a dealer may offer extended coverage. Compare the warranties of the new cars you are considering.

Rustproofing. Buyers of new cars are often offered rustproofing at a cost of $150 to $200. Whether an additional rustproofing compound is necessary is debatable, but consumers have complained about rustproofing jobs that were not done correctly and about warranties that are not honored.

Financing a car

Your first step before shopping should be to determine how much you can afford to spend on a car. Will you pay cash or finance your purchase with a loan? If you are planning to borrow, how much down payment can you afford, what will the interest charge be, and how much will your monthly payment be? Using a loan adds to the cost of the car, but it may be easier than paying out the total purchase price at once. The table below shows the monthly payment you would make for every $1,000 borrowed at various rates of interest over two, three, and four years. Some banks also offer five-year car financing. If you borrow $3,000 for two years at 14%, your monthly payment would be $144.06, i.e., 3 × $48.02.

Years	Interest rates								
	12%	13%	14%	15%	16%	17%	18%	19%	20%
2	$47.08	$47.54	$48.02	$48.48	$48.96	$49.44	$49.92	$50.40	$50.90
3	33.22	33.70	34.18	34.66	35.16	35.66	36.16	36.66	37.16
4	26.34	26.82	27.32	27.82	28.34	28.86	29.38	29.90	30.44

(Figures are for each $1,000 borrowed.)

If you need a loan, check the rates at savings and loan associations and banks. You may be able to get a loan at a slightly lower rate if you belong to a credit union. Dealer's financing is usually more expensive, but those that offer loans through car manufacturer credit companies may have comparable or bargain rates. Some chapters of the American Automobile Association also offer reasonable financing.

Buying a used car

Buying a used car is often more economical than buying a new car. A new car begins to lose value as soon as it is purchased. This decrease in value, or depreciation, takes its greatest toll in the first years of ownership. But while a car's dollar value declines quickly, the car itself may still have many years of use remaining. Also, when you buy a used car, your insurance costs are lower, especially if you elect not to carry collision coverage.

Summer is the peak season for buying a used car and prices are at their highest; you will save money if you shop at another time.

You can get an idea of the prices of used models from the guides mentioned on page 118 and the *Official Used Car Guide* of the National Automobile Dealers Association or the *Kelley Blue Book*. Do not be surprised if the price for a three- or four-year-old car is still close to the original purchase price. Inflation has decreased the value of the dollars you spend.

Summer is the peak season for buying a used car and prices are at their highest; you will save money if you shop at another time.

If you buy from a used-car dealer, look into his or her reputation. Ask friends who have bought cars from that dealer and check the local office of the Better Business Bureau or consumer affairs office for any record of complaints. You may also want to consider buying from a new-car dealer who sells trade-ins or from car-rental companies that sell their cars after a year or so of use. These often come with warranties.

If you buy a used car in a private sale, ask the owner whether a record of car maintenance and repairs has been kept. Cars that have been properly maintained and serviced at regular intervals will outlive neglected autos.

Find out if the manufacturer's warranty is still in effect and whether it can be transferred to you. Ask the seller why he or she is selling the car.

The mileage reading is not a true indication of a car's wear since it may have been altered. Have a mechanic check the car thoroughly before you buy it. An expert will spot problems that you might miss.

Here are other features you can check yourself:

Look at the car in the daylight, or if you must make a quick choice in the evening, take the car into a brightly lit area.

Lift floormats and carpeting to see whether the bottom of the car is in good shape. If it has been in an accident, the floor may show spot welding, or dents or ripples in the metal.

Check doors, trunk, hood, and windows to see that they open and close easily. Doors that do not close properly or sprung trunk or hood locks may indicate that the car has been damaged.

Check the body for evidence of damage or collision: uneven spots in paint, unmatched paint color, scratches, gritty paint surface. Also check for rust spots.

Check bumpers for looseness, indicating damage.

Check tires for wear. When the tread depth reaches $1/16$ inch, tires should be replaced. If front tires show uneven wear, the front end may be out of alignment or the frame may have been damaged in an accident. Also, in a late model car where you see a complete set of replacement tires and a low mileage reading, you have strong evidence that the seller has tampered with the odometer.

If the seller tells you that the tires are original equipment, all four should be of the same make, show similar wear, and have similar serial numbers.

Look for stains around the window area and doors. Stains and a musty odor will be indications that there are body leaks.

Ask whether a jack, lug wrench, and spare tire come with the car. If they do, make sure they fit the car and are operative.

Check the electrical items: lights, air conditioning, heat, radio, defroster, turn signals, wipers, etc.

Make sure the driver's seat can be adjusted. Check the upholstery and carpeting for wear, and see that seatbelts are working.

See that the serial number agrees with the owner's papers.

Check the repair record and gas consumption of each used-car model you are considering. Your local library may have *Consumer Reports* guides which give a repair record and point out serious defects of particular models. There are poor model years and you may want to avoid a car of that brand and year. If you are faced with a decision between two cars, consider the gas consumption of each. For example, say you can buy a 1973 car which costs $1,000 and gets 10 miles to a gallon of gas, or a 1977 car which costs $2,100 and gets 25 miles a

---

Check the repair record and gas consumption of each used-car model you are considering.

---

gallon. Assume further that you travel 15,000 miles a year. You will find that the 1973 car is more costly than the 1977 car when you consider the extra cost of gasoline. Assume that gas costs $1.25 per gallon. The 1973 car will consume 1,500 gallons at an annual cost of $1,875; the 1977 car consumes 600 gallons at a cost of $750. Therefore in just one year, fuel for the 1973 car would cost $1,125 more than gas for the 1977 model ($1,875 − $750). Under these circumstances, the 1977 model is the better buy, although initially it costs $1,100 more.

Leasing a car

Leasing a car is generally not economical for personal driving unless you usually trade in your car after two or three years and you are looking for an alternative to buying. More often, the advantages of leasing cars can be better exploited by businesses.

There are two kinds of car leases. In a closed-end lease, you agree to lease a car for a specified period and return it at the end of the term. This type of lease is also called a walk-away lease or a fixed-cost lease. The amount of your monthly payment depends on the price of the car, how much the company expects to get when it sells the car after you return it, and the maintenance and insurance plans you choose.

An open-end lease is usually a little less expensive but involves more risk since you have a stake in the car's resale value. At the end of the lease period, you can buy the car or have the company sell it for you. If the car sells for more than the leasing company's estimate, you receive the difference. If it sells for less than the estimate, you pay the difference. However, there is a legal limit to how much you have to pay.

. . . the advantages of leasing cars can be better exploited by businesses.

Most leases run for two or three years. If you lease a car, your costs will probably include the charges described below, in addition to the basic monthly payment. The monthly payment takes into account the price of the model and the lessor's estimate of depreciation, interest cost, overhead, and profit.

Most lessors ask a security deposit equal to one or two months' lease payments. This deposit is returned at the end of the term provided the car is in good shape. One monthly payment may also be required in advance. Make sure that this amount is not a down payment which increases your total cost.

Monthly payments are subject to sales tax, and you will probably have to pay registration fees. Some companies will do the paperwork for you and include the cost in their charges.

You will have to pay for insurance, though your rate may be lower through the leasing company than you could obtain through your own insurance company. Under the leasing agreement, you will probably have to carry substantial liability coverage.

Maintenance may be your responsibility or the company may offer a maintenance and service plan for an added monthly charge. Such plans may pay for some or all maintenance costs, but usually will not cover any damage resulting from an accident, collision, or driver abuse.

A lease may specify that you will be responsible for damage and missing equipment discovered at the end of the lease period.

The cost of a lease will vary with the final mileage on the car. The leasing company asks for an estimate of how many miles you expect to drive the car each year and bases its charges on that figure. If you drive more than that number, the company will impose a surcharge of a few cents per mile.

If you are considering leasing a car, review these costs. By comparing them with the cost and interest charges for a new car, you can determine which is a better choice for you. By law, a lease agreement must specify all costs in writing, and the company must tell you what insurance is required, how you or the company may cancel the lease and what penalty may be charged, the penalty for late payments or default, who is responsible for maintenance, and whether you can buy the car at the end of the lease and how the purchase price will be determined.

Keeping your old car

If you have owned your present car for a few years, you probably have reached a crossroad: Do you continue to maintain your old car or do you sell it and buy a new one? If you have had to put several hundred dollars into the car and you

---

As a general rule, assuming that your present car is paid off, the cost of repairing the old car is less than the finance charges of a new car.

---

can also foresee upcoming expenses, such as a new set of tires, you may be inclined to unload the car now. It may appear that a new car with a good warranty would be more economical, but consider these points:

As a general rule, assuming that your present car is paid off, the cost of repairing the old car is less than the finance charges of a new car. For example, if you have to finance $5,000 over four years at 17%, your annual payments would exceed $1,700 a year; $1,700 can cover substantial repairs on an old car. Of course, if you keep your old car, you must be prepared to pay a large repair bill on the spot whereas new-car payments are fixed and spread out evenly.

Experts generalize that the major repairs for a car occur in years three, seven, and ten.

Compare general operating costs of both the old and proposed new car. If your old car is a gas guzzler while the new model is gas efficient and you drive more than 10,000 miles annually, fuel savings will offset the cost of a new car. Say you normally drive 1,500 miles a month and your old car gets 15 miles to the gallon. If you pay $1.25 a gallon, your current monthly gas costs are $125. If you buy a car that gets 30 miles to the gallon, you would cut your monthly costs in half and be ahead $62.50 each month. Of course, you must figure the difference in gasoline prices; an old car may use less expensive regular gasoline whereas a new car usually requires the more expensive unleaded type.

Two factors that cannot be ignored are personal temperament and taste. An old car may be less dependable and may require more time in the shop. Experts generalize that the major repairs for a car occur in years three, seven, and ten. If you have already come through a major repair year, you may be temporarily freed from time at the service station, but there are no guarantees. Also, the attractiveness of your car may be an important consideration to you. Outmoded styling may be a sufficient reason for you to buy a new model over cost economy.

Finally, the decision to keep an old car means that the day of purchasing a new car has merely been delayed. The old car will not last forever and new car prices keep rising. The purchase of a new car now ensures at least several years of generally worry-free ownership. The future with an old car is uncertain.

Selling your old car

If you decide that when buying a new car you do not want to trade in your old car, you have two options: you can sell your car privately or you can sell it to a used-car dealer. You will get your best price selling it privately.

Start by checking the *Kelley Blue Book* for the present value of your car. Depending on the model, you can usually get from $300 to $1,000 more than *Blue Book* value for a used car in a private sale. Also, check different newspapers in your area for advertisements for cars of the same year and model. See how much others are asking for their cars (keep in mind that the prices asked are not necessarily the prices received). If you have low mileage on your car considering its age, you may be able to sell it for more than one with higher mileage. If the body is in good shape (no dents or rust, and few paint chips), you may command an even higher price.

It is advisable to set your asking price a bit above what you will actually settle for.

Decide which newspapers or special journals will give your ad the best coverage. Consider your audience. If you are trying to sell a used sportscar for $8,500, you should advertise in media with a higher-income readership. In some areas, radio stations read ads for secondhand items, including cars and trucks. Their coverage is broad and they often have a loyal following. Check rates and "package deals." Some newspapers will let you place an ad for three days (for example, Wednesday, Friday, and Sunday) for a reduced rate. Keep your ad short, but include all pertinent facts, such as model, year, mileage, special features and options, condition, and price.

It is advisable to set your asking price a bit above what you will actually settle for. Buyers of secondhand items like to "bargain" so you should give yourself some leeway. Be sure you set your desired price at a realistic, not an overly inflated level.

Once you have a buyer for your car, make sure that you are paid either in cash (for which you should give a written receipt) or by a certified or bank check. Do not accept a personal check or money order. If you are still paying off a bank note on the car and the bank holds a lien against it, you should pay off the note immediately so the bank will release its lien. This is especially important if the buyer of your car is financing it through a bank. He or she will not be able to obtain financing if there is an outstanding lien against the car.

When you sell your car, you must sign the transfer section of your registration card and turn it over to the buyer. You must also furnish the buyer with a bill of sale and the certificate of title; he will need these to register the car in his name. Keep copies of all checks and receipts.

You will probably choose to remove your license plates from your old car and use them on your new one. However, if you have ordered new plates, you must turn in the old ones at the Department of Motor Vehicles and may be entitled to a credit.

Selling your car to a used-car dealer is an advantage only if you are pressed for time. He will offer you cash on the spot if he wants your car. However, his price will be far lower than you can get in a private sale because he must, in turn, figure his cost to hold it in inventory and his profit margin, and re-sell it.

It is especially important to know the approximate value of your car on the used-car market if you sell to a dealer. Many will try to convince you that your car is not salable for one reason or another, to try to get you to accept a lower price. On the other hand there is an occasional used-car dealer who will tell you he cannot give you nearly as much as you could get in a private sale.

Chapter 7

BUYING OR SELLING A HOUSE, CONDOMINIUM, OR COOPERATIVE APARTMENT

OWNING a home is still part of the American dream. Unfortunately, for first-time buyers the dream is increasingly hard to realize because of inflated real estate values and high mortgage interest rates. Those who can muster the cash for a down payment on a home are finding that their money buys less house; expectations must be compromised.

This chapter discusses new ways to finance a home and offers pointers for sellers who wish to profit from today's high real estate values.

Owning a home is still part of the American dream.

Co-ops and condominiums are gaining in popularity as a home choice, though in some cases conversion of existing rental apartments by landlords forces the "choice" on tenants. The rights and options of tenants are explained in this chapter.

Tax advantages of buying a home

The tax laws favor home ownership over renting. You may not deduct the rent on your personal residence, whereas if you own your home you may deduct:

1. Interest paid on the mortgage.
2. Real estate taxes.
3. Uninsured casualty damage to your property.

These deductions reduce the actual cost of home ownership. For example, say you are in the 34% income tax bracket and you have the choice of paying $550 a month in rent or $700 in mortgage payments (most of which is interest in the early years) and real estate taxes. The rental is a more expensive choice. Why? Because the $700 in payments entitles you to a tax deduction worth $238. Thus your out-of-pocket cost is actually $462 ($700 − $238).

When you sell your home, all or part of the gain may be tax free. If you are age 55 or over, you may elect to avoid tax on gain (up to $125,000). If you are under 55, or 55 or over and do not want to elect to avoid tax, you may defer tax by buying or building a new home within two years before or after sale of your old house at a cost at least equal to the amount you received from the sale of the old house. If you do not qualify for deferral, your gain will be taxed at capital gain rates if you held the house long term.

How much house can you afford?

A house is expensive to maintain. Not only are there fixed expenses, such as your mortgage payments (which include principal repayments and interest), real estate taxes, and insurance, but there are also monthly expenses that vary, such as utilities, water, and perhaps garbage collection. Finally, there is the constant, though unpredictable, cost of repairs and maintenance, from the inexpensive leaky faucet to the high-priced new roof.

The Federal Housing Administration and the Veterans Administration use two guidelines for determining how much house you can carry, based on your income:

1. Mortgage payments (principal and interest) and real estate taxes must be less than 28% of pre-tax monthly income.
2. Mortgage payments and real estate taxes plus other monthly debts must be no more than 36% of pre-tax monthly income.

In the final analysis, you must decide how much you can put into a house each month. Lifestyle and financial obligations vary.

Old house vs. new house

Whether to buy a new or older home is largely a matter of personal taste and availability in the area where you are looking. Here are some points to consider:

When you buy and move into a new house, you find everything fresh, clean, and modern. You may even have the opportunity to choose paint, wallpaper, flooring, and fixtures, but only up to the amount the builder has allowed for these items. If you want features that cost more than the builder's allowances, they will be installed at your expense.

Builders of new houses usually provide a lawn, but no landscaping. Nor do they include screens, storm windows, or storm doors. You will have to take these expenses into consideration over and above your down payment. You may also have to weather the frustrations of "bugs" in construction.

A new house is more easily financed than an older house. . . . Banks may require smaller down payments for new houses than on comparable older homes.

When a house is new, and until it is "broken in," doors and windows may stick, outside steps may crack, heating and hot water systems may need adjustments, and as the house settles, it may need repainting, sealing of cracks, or tile repairs in bathrooms.

A new house is more easily financed than an older house. Builders who have overbuilt may offer financing assistance to reduce their inventory. Banks may require smaller down payments for new houses than on comparable older homes.

Buying an older house also has advantages. It usually has a warmth, charm, and at least the appearance of sturdiness not found in new homes at comparable prices. An older home will probably save you the expenses of lawn seeding, landscaping, screens, and storm windows and doors. In a well-established neighborhood, schools are not as likely to become overcrowded as quickly as in new development areas. Property taxes will probably not increase as quickly as in growing, new communities. However, an older house may need modernization, particularly in the kitchen and bathroom. Walls may have to be removed to enlarge bedrooms or create a family room. Chances are that you will want to repaint or redecorate. Rewiring may be necessary to accommodate all your electric appliances. If all these expenses make the cost of an old house more than a comparable new one, and you do not have the ready cash for modernization, it would not be wise to buy the older house. Alternatively, if you can live with the house as it is or can do much of the work yourself, you may pick up a bargain—a "handyman's special."

There is one other consideration you should not overlook: make certain the older house is in a neighborhood that is not deteriorating or becoming commercial in character. If it is, your chances of getting your investment back will not be as good as if you bought a comparably priced new house in an up-and-coming residential area.

In your search for a family home, you may find one that meets nearly all your requirements—except, for example, that it has no family room and no master bedroom and bathroom. The price of the house is low enough to allow you to add the three rooms. The property appears large enough to accommodate the expansion. Nevertheless, before you bind yourself to any purchase, make sure that the enlargement will not encroach beyond the building line and will meet legal limits.

Check that the necessary permits for construction will be granted by the local authorities. Ask the present owner for the property survey, showing the limits of the land you are purchasing. Consult the local zoning and building authorities. Ask them whether you would be allowed to proceed with your project.

When you get title and are ready to proceed with your expansion project, you will need an architect, plans, and a contractor, just as if you were constructing a custom-built house.

Check list on buying a home

You may find two or three houses in the right price range, each of which meets most of your requirements. However, none may meet all of them. You must make a comparison of the favorable and unfavorable features of each and then make your decision. Here is a check list of some points to weigh:

Size and expansion possibilities. If the number of rooms is adequate now but might not be in a few years, is there room for expansion? Will zoning laws permit you to expand the house?

Topography of the lot. Is there sufficient level ground for the recreation area you require? Will abutting property make a retaining wall necessary? Is drainage adequate?

Public utilities. Will you have to maintain a well, or does the public authority supply water? Is garbage and trash removal a public service? Are the roads near the house kept clear of snow and ice by a public service? What are the zoning laws in the immediate and neighboring vicinity? A home near an area zoned for commercial or industrial use will not be as desirable on a resale, and will depreciate more quickly in value.

Is the house near a traffic center, a main highway, or a transportation center? Traffic noises make a home less desirable on a resale. Weigh this against the advantages of easy travel to work and shopping. What is the cost for public transportation to work, shopping areas, and places of entertainment and recreation?

Will you need a second car for daily travel?

Is the house within walking distance of schools, place of worship, playgrounds, and shopping areas?

Are there sidewalks for children who walk to school?

Do zoning laws protect the neighborhood from deteriorating?

Will your children be bused to schools at a distance from your home? Check the location of the school your children will be eligible to attend. You may choose a house because of the high educational standards of a nearby school, only to find out that your address is in another school district. Check with the school about availability of transportation. Your home may not be within the distance limit for school bus service.

Are there sewers or other public improvements in the area for which your house is likely to be assessed?

Have you gone into and around the house on rainy days to look for water seepage and cracks in masonry around window sills and in the basement?

Will your car(s) fit into the driveway or garage?

Is the electricity amperage adequate for the electric dryer, air conditioners, and other equipment you may wish to install?

Is the water pressure adequate?

Is the heating and hot water system a costly type? Is it in good condition?

Are other houses in the neighborhood maintained with pride of ownership or are they rundown?

Is the neighborhood stabilized or improving?

Do the grounds require immediate lawn work or landscaping, a retaining wall?

Is the price comparable to sales prices of similar homes in the area?

Is the type of house one that is readily salable?

Initial purchase costs

In addition to cash for a down payment, count on these initial expenses, also referred to as "closing costs," when figuring how much cash you will need for a home purchase.

Home inspection. An inspection of your prospective home by a qualified engineer or home inspection company is essential. The lending institution may also require it. You need a report on the condition of the roof, water system, sewage, general construction, and major repairs that can be anticipated immediately or in the near future. Inspection may reveal termite damage or other defects which might preclude your buying the property or serve as a basis for renegotiating the purchase price. The cost of an inspection may run a few hundred dollars, but it may prevent you from buying a home with potentially disastrous and costly faults.

Survey. A lending institution is likely to insist on a survey which would reveal any encroachments against the boundary lines of the land—as might happen if a neighbor put up a fence or shrubs along property lines. If you are buying a house that the seller has owned for only a few years, the bank may accept his or her survey.

Title company insurance. Generally required by a lender, a title company insurance policy certifies the seller's title for the lender. A buyer may also want similar insurance. The cost of title and mortgage insurance depends primarily on the amount of insurance protection and location of the home.

Expenses of obtaining a mortgage. Additional expenses may include an appraisal fee paid to the lender; expenses of its attorney for drawing the mortgage and other legal papers; recording fees, usually nominal, paid to the county; and any mortgage tax levied by the state. You may also be required to pay "points." A point is 1% of the mortgage. Thus if you are getting a $60,000 mortgage and must pay two points, the charge is $1,200 ($600 × 2). Points are explained in detail later in this chapter.

Lawyer's fees. Before engaging an attorney, ask the fee for representing you at the closing of title. If you think the fee is high, check with another attorney. When buying a condo, engage a lawyer who is thoroughly knowledgeable in this highly specialized and relatively new field of law.

Adjustments for advance payments. On the closing of title, certain adjustments are made on taxes and insurance premiums. When an existing mortgage is assumed, interest must be adjusted. You must generally be prepared to pay in advance up to six months' real estate taxes and, to protect the lender, insurance premiums up to three years.

Fuel adjustments. If the house has oil heat, the buyer must pay for the oil in the tank. With the cost of oil today, this could run to several hundred dollars.

A related item which you should not ignore is the cost of moving. Whether you move yourself with a rented truck or pay a professional mover, you must allocate the necessary funds.

Financing your home with a mortgage

The purchase price of your house or condo, over and above the cash down payment, is generally financed by a mortgage. The lender is the mortgagee; you are the mortgagor. In consideration for the money advanced to you to pay the balance of the seller's price, you pledge the house and land as security for repayment of your loan with interest. If you fail to pay your mortgage debt, the mortgagee may foreclose, that is, sell your house in order to pay off the mortgage debt.

The size of the mortgage you can obtain depends on the availability of money in the market, your credit, the age and condition of the house and its current market value, the number of years over which the loan is to be repaid, and the rate of interest.

There are several sources for mortgage funds. Mortgage money can be obtained from commercial or savings banks, savings and loan associations, life insurance companies, and other lenders, such as relatives or other individuals. Some states are moving to allow state employee pension funds to offer low-cost mortgages. The types of mortgages currently available are discussed later in this chapter.

The size of the mortgage you can obtain depends on such factors as the availability of money in the market, your credit, the age and condition of the house and its current market value, the number of years over which the loan is to be repaid, and the rate of interest.

Mortgage rates and the amount of down payment required vary by area of the country. Rates may also favor new houses compared with previously occupied houses.

You may have to pay "points" to get a mortgage. Points are paid by the buyer as a way of compensating the lender for the cost of money. On a FHA/VA loan, the seller may have to pay the points difference in a lump sum; the price of the house is raised correspondingly.

You must shop around for a mortgage to get the best deal. In the past you could call ten banks and probably be quoted the same terms. Not so today. Rates vary, types of mortgages vary, terms vary. You may have to call 20 or more banks to get an overview of available mortgages. Be aware, however, that some banks will lend only to their customers. If you do not have an account with the bank, you will not get a loan, regardless of your credit rating or earnings.

Types of mortgages

In the past few years the mortgage field has been adapting to a changing economy. As a prospective buyer, you may be confronted with various types of mortgages, many devised as a response to inflated values, high interest rates, and tight mortgage money.

Conventional mortgage. With a conventional, or fixed-rate, mortgage your monthly payment is fixed throughout the life of the loan, which may run to 25 or 30 years. At the beginning of the loan, most of the payment is interest charges; at the end of the loan, most of the payment is principal.

. . . the mortgage field has been adapting to a changing economy.

Example:
You get an $80,000, 30-year mortgage at 15%. Your monthly payment (principal repayment and interest) is $759.

Adjustable-rate mortgage (ARM). The interest rate on the mortgage fluctuates according to an index tied to either U.S. Treasury securities, money market rates, the Federal Home Loan Bank Board's average for mortgage rates, or another index. How often the rate can be adjusted will vary from state to state and whether the bank is governed by federal regulations. The change in rates may translate into an adjustment in

MONTHLY MORTGAGE PAYMENTS ON 30-YEAR LOAN

Mortgage Amount	10½%	11%	11½%	12%	12½%	13%	13½%	14%	14½%	15%	15½%	16%	17%	18%
$ 10,000	$ 91	$ 95	$ 99	$ 103	$ 107	$ 111	$ 115	$ 118	$ 122	$ 126	$ 130	$ 134	$ 143	$ 151
$ 12,000	110	114	119	123	128	133	137	142	147	152	157	161	171	181
$ 16,000	146	152	158	165	170	177	183	190	196	202	209	215	228	241
$ 20,000	183	190	198	206	213	221	229	237	245	253	261	269	285	301
$ 24,000	220	229	238	247	256	265	275	284	294	303	313	323	342	362
$ 28,000	256	267	277	288	299	310	321	332	343	354	365	377	399	422
$ 32,000	293	305	317	329	341	354	366	379	392	405	417	430	456	482
$ 36,000	329	343	357	370	384	398	412	427	441	455	470	484	513	543
$ 40,000	366	381	396	411	427	442	458	474	490	506	522	538	570	603
$ 44,000	403	419	436	453	469	487	504	521	539	556	574	592	627	663
$ 48,000	439	457	475	494	512	531	550	569	588	607	626	645	684	723
$ 52,000	476	495	515	535	555	575	595	616	637	658	678	699	741	784
$ 56,000	512	533	555	576	598	619	641	664	686	708	731	753	798	844
$ 60,000	549	571	594	617	640	664	687	711	735	759	783	807	855	904
$ 64,000	585	610	634	658	683	708	733	758	784	809	835	861	912	965
$ 68,000	622	648	673	699	726	752	779	806	833	860	887	914	969	1025
$ 72,000	659	686	713	741	768	796	824	853	882	910	939	968	1026	1085
$ 76,000	695	724	753	782	811	841	870	900	931	961	991	1022	1084	1145
$ 80,000	732	762	792	823	854	885	916	948	980	1012	1044	1076	1141	1206
$ 84,000	768	800	832	864	896	929	962	995	1029	1062	1096	1130	1198	1266
$ 88,000	805	838	871	905	939	973	1008	1043	1078	1113	1148	1183	1256	1326
$ 92,000	842	876	911	946	982	1018	1053	1090	1127	1163	1200	1237	1312	1387
$ 96,000	878	914	951	987	1024	1062	1099	1137	1176	1214	1252	1291	1367	1447
$100,000	915	952	990	1029	1067	1106	1145	1185	1225	1264	1305	1345	1426	1507

NOTE: All figures have been rounded to the nearest dollar.

monthly payments or it may affect the outstanding loan balance. A borrower may find that ARMs are being offered at a slightly lower initial rate than a conventional mortgage or with fewer points. Check on the limits to which interest and/or monthly payments may be raised.

Adjustable mortgage loan (AML). An AML is the same as an ARM but offered by federally chartered savings banks and S&Ls. *Variable-rate mortgages (VRM)* are similar in that interest rates could vary. However, because of the stringent limitation on rate fluctuations, few banks are now offering VRMs. A variation on the VRM is the Wachovia adjustable mortgage created by a North Carolina bank. This is how it works: Initial payments on a 30-year loan are figured at the prevailing rate. Payments are fixed for five years but the rate is recomputed every quarter. An account is kept of how much of each payment is applied to principal and how much to interest, based on the changing rate. Every five years, monthly payments are readjusted (up or down as much as 25%, more than 25% after 25 years) to ensure that the principal will be paid off on time.

Graduated-payment mortgage (GMP). Monthly payments increase according to a schedule set at the beginning of the loan. This type of mortgage is designed to make financing more affordable by keeping monthly payments low in the first few years of the loan. The price of this reduction to the home buyer may be negative amortization. That is, instead of reducing the outstanding principal, the borrower may be increasing it for the first three, five, or even ten years. This means that if a house bought with an initial $50,000 mortgage is sold after two years, the borrower would have to repay *more* than $50,000.

Shared-appreciation mortgage (SAM). This new type of loan may change the character of home ownership. With a SAM, the homeowner is in partnership with the lender, either a bank or a private investor. The borrower gets a reduced interest rate in exchange for promising to share the profits with the lender when the house is sold. This is a concept similar to "sharing equity," where an investor furnishes the down payment and the homeowner occupies the house and pays the carrying charges; at a set date the house is refinanced (or sold) and the lender receives the equity plus a share of the appreciation.

Rollover mortgage (ROM). The mortgage looks like a conventional mortgage as monthly payments are fixed for the life of the loan. However, there is this catch: a ROM must be refinanced every few years, often three or five, at the then-prevailing interest rate. In fact, monthly payments are set only until refinancing is required.

Renegotiable mortgage or balloon-payment mortgage. This loan is similar to a ROM in that the principal must be repaid at the end of a set term by refinancing. However, unlike the ROM, there may be no guarantee of refinancing.

Creative financing. This is a catch-all phrase for combining a variety of financing techniques to cover the purchase price. One device is for the buyer to assume the seller's outstanding mortgage. The buyer takes over the mortgage and continues to pay off the lender. The buyer pays the seller the difference between the price of the house and the outstanding balance of the mortgage. However, since the assumable mortgages result in a lower return to lending institutions, they are being phased out by a new banking law passed in 1982.

Another device is the purchase-money mortgage. If you cannot get financing to buy the house you want, the seller might take a mortgage on the house if he or she is not in immediate need of funds to buy another residence. The purchase-money mortgage may be for the entire cost of the home in excess of a down payment or in addition to a mortgage secured through a bank or other institution. Sometimes, a purchase-money mortgage requires a balloon payment shortly after the sale. For example, you may buy a $100,000 house by putting down $10,000 cash, obtaining a $75,000 mortgage from the bank and getting a purchase-money mortgage from the seller for $15,000. This loan may contain a clause that the $15,000 is due 12 months from the date of sale. If you do not come up with the cash or refinance, the seller may foreclose on the house.

Another financing arrangement sometimes accompanying new home purchases is a "buy down," in which the builder pays the lender a lump sum to lower the buyer's monthly payments for the first few years of the mortgage.

Federal Housing Administration mortgage. The FHA, a division of the Department of Housing and Urban Development (HUD), does not loan mortgage money directly. An FHA mortgage is obtained from a private lending institution, but the FHA insures the lender against loss in case of the homeowner's default. Because of this guarantee, some lenders may be willing to accept smaller down payments and a lower interest rate, and may lend their money over longer periods. However, when mortgage money is tight, lending institutions are less inclined to handle loans insured by the FHA. FHA charges a low insurance premium on the unpaid balance, included in the monthly payments called for by the mortgage. There is a dollar limitation on the value of the homes for which the FHA will provide mortgage insurance.

If you apply for an FHA-insured mortgage, the FHA will make a complete review of your ability to meet the mortgage obligations even after the bank has run its credit check and approved you for the loan. In addition to appraising the property, the FHA will consider your estimated continuing, dependable income; estimated prospective monthly housing expenses; and estimated living costs, debts, and other financial obligations. Thus an FHA mortgage will take more time for approval than a conventional one.

Veterans Administration mortgage. If you are a veteran, you should check with the local VA branch regarding eligibility and opportunity for a VA-guaranteed mortgage. Generally, a VA mortgage will run for a longer term, may have lower interest rates, and require a smaller down payment, or none in some circumstances. As with FHA loans, those insured by the VA are only granted for property meeting rigid standards.

Other mortgage terms

Escrow and insurance. In addition to interest and amortization payments, the mortgagee may require you to pay a stated amount each month toward real property taxes into an "escrow account" from which taxes will be paid by the mortgagee. This monthly payment is subject to change if taxes are increased. You must count on this, too, as a carrying charge of owning your home.

The terms of the mortgage will require you to maintain adequate fire insurance (at least enough to protect the lender's interest), keep the house in good repair, and pay taxes promptly (where the bank itself does not take over this responsibility through an escrow arrangement). Homeowner's insurance is discussed further in Chapter 9.

Prepayment. When negotiating for a mortgage, it is advisable to request the privilege of prepaying it, preferably without a penalty. Some lending institutions may not allow you to prepay a mortgage. Some will allow prepayment on receipt of a penalty fee which is a percentage of the unpaid balance due. Some may charge a prepayment penalty only during the first 12 or 18 months of the mortgage. If the interest rate on your mortgage is below the current rate, the mortgagee might waive the penalty and gladly accept prepayments.

Negotiating the price and going to contract

A house may be advertised for a sale price of $150,000. This is not necessarily the price at which it will sell. Various factors affect the price: how long the house has been on the market; general demand in the area; whether the sellers are under pressure to sell; and the real estate market in general.

There are no absolutes in negotiating a price. Do not lose sight of your objective and do not let a small difference in price between you and the seller prevent you from reaching an agreement.

If you are dealing directly with the owner of the house, negotiations should be straightforward. You make an offer of what you think the house is worth and what you think the seller may accept. The seller will either respond with a counteroffer or will tell you that the asking price is "firm" and no less will be accepted. Then you must decide whether you will submit another offer or decline to continue negotiations.

If you are dealing through a real estate broker, negotiations are less direct and may be more complicated. You relate your offering price to the broker who relays your bid to the seller. The seller's response comes back to you via the broker. Be aware that while the broker may be helping you to buy a house, the broker's commission generally around 6% is dependent on the final selling price. A higher sales price means a bigger commission.

Once you and the seller have agreed on a price, you may be asked for a "binder." A "binder," typically 1% of the purchase price, is dispensed with in certain localities but required in others. The binder is usually held by the seller until you have had the house inspected by an engineer. By accepting

---

. . . while the broker may be helping you to buy a house, the broker's commission generally around 6% is dependent on the final selling price.

---

the binder, the seller will not accept additional bids on the house. If the inspection is unsatisfactory, your binder will usually be returned. Whether you lose the binder if you do not go through with the purchase depends on a number of factors, such as the law or custom in your locality and whether you have proceeded so slowly that it caused the seller harm.

Once you are certain you want to proceed, consult a lawyer who will assist you in the final stages of buying the home. The seller's lawyer will draw up the contract. Ask the seller to have his lawyer get in touch with yours, and the contract can be signed within a few days. At that time you make your down payment, typically 10% of the purchase price, but you and the seller may agree to different terms.

Once you are certain you want to proceed, consult a lawyer who will assist you in the final stages of buying the home.

Your lawyer will see that all the terms and conditions of sale are included in the written agreement. If your purchase is dependent on getting a mortgage, your lawyer will include that condition in your contract. If the seller offers carpeting, curtains, appliances, or garden equipment with the house, your lawyer will see that you get title to this personal property at the closing.

The contract will also contain a "closing date," that is, a date when you are to take title. How fixed is the closing date? Generally, it is flexible, but if you are unable to close within a few weeks of the stated date, you may be subject to a penalty —or worse, lose your down payment.

Some home buyers are under the impression that the attorney representing the lender will look out for their interests as well, and that a lawyer is an unnecessary expense. This is not so. The lawyer for the mortgagee is there to protect the lending institution, not you. If there is an encroachment or easement discovered on the title examination, your interest as owner could be affected, but that will not deter the lender from giving you the mortgage. The mortgagee's interest for the amount it advances will be adequately secured despite this encroachment. However, the marketability of your title might be affected. If there is an open assessment against the property, the mortgagee's attorney will not be concerned about who pays it, or even if it is paid. But your lawyer will try to get the seller to pay at least a part.

If the seller has failed to complete certain work called for by the contract as of the closing date, the attorney for the lender may not be concerned; but your lawyer will work to protect your interests. Your attorney should try either to have part of the purchase price put "in escrow" pending the seller's performance, or make some other arrangement for your protection, or obtain an agreement that the seller can have the balance in escrow provided the work is completed on or before a certain date. On the seller's default, the money would go to you to have the work done. If the seller has made representations about construction, your lawyer will try to get them in writing.

Your attorney can also find out whether the house you are buying is protected by FHA or VA rules obligating the builder to correct structural defects, or to make allowances for the costs of repairs.

An attorney is also essential to other real estate transactions, especially the purchase of a condominium or cooperative apartment. Legal advice is also needed in the purchase of a mobile home and its lot.

Should you use a real estate broker to buy or sell?

Generally, you do not pay any fee when you consult a broker about buying a house because broker commissions are payable by the seller when the house is sold. However, in some parts of the country, you may find brokers who act only on the buyer's behalf. For the services of such a broker, you pay an hourly or flat fee or a percentage of the sale price. Consulting a local broker, who generally knows most of the houses on the market in the area, will save you a lot of time and energy and expedite your search for a home that meets your requirements. A broker may also know which lending institutions will finance the purchase of the house you choose, what the lending institutions look for in issuing credit on mortgages, how much an institution is likely to lend, and where you can get an FHA- or VA-insured mortgage, if you qualify. A broker should also be able to assist in "creative financing" to swing a purchase. Brokers are generally more expert than laymen in the art of negotiation and know how to keep the channels of communication open after a buyer's low offer is rejected by the seller.

On the other hand, do not be overly swayed by a broker's sales pitch or enthusiasm for the house. Remember that the broker is essentially the seller's agent and will be paid only when a sale is consummated. If you see a house advertised "by owner," it means that no broker is involved. If you deal directly with the owner and do not have broker's fees to consider, you are in effect getting more house for your money.

Consulting a local broker will save you a lot of time and energy and expedite your search for a home.

Should you sell your house through a broker or should you do it yourself? There are many factors to consider:

If you decide to sell your house through a broker, be aware of the services you are entitled to under your agreement. For the price of the commission, usually 6%–7% of the final selling price, the broker agrees to advertise and show your house.

The house may also be publicized in a multiple-listing service. If you sign an exclusive right-to-sell agreement, which typically runs for 90 days, you must pay the broker's commission even if you sell the house yourself without the broker's help within this period. If you do not consent to such an agreement,

---

Selling the house yourself has one big advantage: you save on broker's commissions. On a $100,000 house you could save $6,000 to $7,000.

---

the broker may be less than enthusiastic about showing your house. The broker should be able to help you set a price by informing you of recent sales of comparable houses in the area. Your price should be realistic, allowing for the payment of broker's commissions and some room for negotiation with the buyer.

Selling the house yourself has one big advantage: you save on broker's commissions. On a $100,000 house you could save $6,000 to $7,000. However, if you do not use a broker, you must advertise properly and be available to show your house. Look in your local papers for house advertisements and note which ones catch your eye. In writing your own ad, list the essentials of your house, emphasizing its good points, and use the style of the ad which piqued your interest. When you show your house, prepare a fact sheet to give to prospective buyers. On this sheet you can list, room by room, what items you are selling with the house, as well as house and property specifications (lot size, method of heating, annual taxes). Under your state's law, you may be required to provide, at the buyer's request, your energy bills for the past two years. Be prepared to spend a great deal of time showing prospective buyers around your home. Many who come to look are just curious; only a few will be serious about buying. Once you have a firm offer, you should still continue to show the house (with the buyer's knowledge) and to take backup offers in case the first buyer is unable to get a mortgage. Remember that a broker has a pool of buyers in case one deal falls through, but you have only those who have been attracted by your advertisement, or those who have heard by word-of-mouth that your house is for sale.

Buying a home if you are single

Buying a home is not exclusively a dream of married couples; many singles are homeowners or would-be owners. The investment opportunity and tax advantages of home ownership apply equally for singles. For some singles, such as young professionals without children, the marketplace is broader than for couples with children. Not restricted by school districts, some singles have been opting for home ownership in inner cities rather than the suburbs. The revitalization of some urban centers is in part due to the commitment of singles to their homes and cities.

It is not easy to buy a home on one income. In response to the housing squeeze of the 1980s, one solution for many singles seeking a decent, affordable place to live is to share a house. An increasingly popular practice is for unrelated singles to buy a house together that they could not afford on their own.

Anyone considering sharing a house should have a lawyer draw up an agreement specifying how costs, such as down payment, mortgage, utilities, and repairs, will be divided.

Young working singles sometimes find a shared house more economical and comfortable than an apartment. Some home builders, noting this trend, are designing homes to be shared, including features such as two master bedrooms and large central kitchens. These are called "tandem" homes.

Buying a home with one or more persons complicates legal and financial matters. Anyone considering sharing a house should have a lawyer draw up an agreement specifying how costs, such as down payment, mortgage, utilities, and repairs, will be divided. The agreement should provide for possible problems in the future. What happens if one person decides to move out, becomes ill, loses his or her job, or dies? In addition, the contract should state whether anyone else, for example, a friend or relative of one owner, may also live in the house.

Home buyers can choose the form of ownership they prefer. Joint tenants share equally in the ownership of the house, and if one tenant dies the house automatically passes to the other. For tenants in common, each person's interest in the property depends on his or her financial contribution, and each person can sell, mortgage, or give away his or her interest without the consent of the other tenants unless they sign a legal agreement beforehand prohibiting such actions. In case of death, a tenant can bequeath his or her share of the property to anyone. Individuals can also form a partnership to buy a house with details spelled out in a partnership agreement. In case of death, the partnership retains title to the property, although a tenant may bequeath his or her interest to someone outside the partnership.

Financing a home can be harder for unrelated individuals, but the Equal Credit Opportunity Act provides some support by prohibiting institutions from turning down a loan application because of marital status. Nevertheless, some lenders are a little wary of shared-home owners and view them as credit risks simply because they form a new group in the market.

According to some economists, home sharing and other adjustments to the changing housing situation are permanent changes, not temporary solutions. While they admit that the American dream of owning one's own home is still extremely strong, they predict that it may have to be revised under economic pressures.

Condominium and cooperative home ownership

Today, condominium or cooperative dwellings are alternatives to the single-family home or rental apartment. They offer the equity and tax features of single-family home ownership without the burdens of upkeep or high taxes that single-family home ownership entails.

In recent years, the conversion of rental units into condos and co-ops has accelerated greatly. Even if you had not been considering home ownership, you may be forced to move or to buy the apartment you are now renting. The availability of reasonably priced rental units is disappearing in many areas of the country, adding to the pressure to buy. Even if you are not currently considering a purchase, you should familiarize yourself with condo or co-op ownership to avoid a panic buy should your apartment be converted.

Condominium ownership. When you buy a condominium, you own your unit and with other owners become a part owner of common areas such as halls and elevators. Also, you own in part the hidden elements, such as the plumbing and electrical wiring. Grounds, pools, recreation and parking areas are yours in part. The monthly maintenance fee you pay ensures upkeep of the common areas and spares you the chores of garden care and snow removal, and also may provide security at a gate or lobby. Some repairs to your unit may be included in the maintenance fee, but generally you must handle the cost yourself. Typically, utilities are your responsibility, though in some condos and cooperatives maintenance charges are higher because these costs are included.

Cooperative ownership. If you buy into a co-op, you buy shares in the building management. Your shares are applied to your unit, but you do not actually own your unit. As in a condominium, you pay a monthly maintenance fee.

Note that some banks have more stringent terms on a mortgage for a condo or loan for a co-op than on a single-family home mortgage.

In a co-op residents share all costs, which means greater liability than in a condominium. If new bills arise or a resident defaults, all shareholders must pay part of the amount. However, broad liability insurance may offer some protection to residents and building directors.

Tax benefits. The tax advantages of condo ownership are the same as those for single-family houses. Mortgage interest and property taxes are deductible. Property taxes are based on an owner's percentage of common elements and are assessed on each unit. Tax breaks are also enjoyed by co-op sharehold-

ers; a proportionate share of taxes and interest can be deducted. The extent of your tax advantages and liabilities must
be carefully examined in regard to a particular purchase and
current law. Get professional advice here.

Financing. Financing the purchase of a condo or co-op is
similar to financing a single-family home. The same sources for
mortgages are available. For a co-op, you must take out a personal loan. Technically, it is not a mortgage since you own
shares instead of property, but cooperative loans are otherwise similar to mortgages. Interest rates for cooperative loans
may be the same or slightly higher than the rates for mortgages, depending on the financial institution; as with a mortgage, you may be required to pay points. Note that some banks
have more stringent terms on a mortgage for a condo or loan
for a co-op than on a single-family home mortgage.

Condo or co-op management

Initially, a developer or sponsor runs the condo or co-op,
but as units or shares are sold an association of owners takes
over. It handles the maintenance fees, collects from slow pay-
ers, enforces the rules, and through its treasurer (or an accounting firm) pays insurance premiums, taxes, bills, and
salaries. In larger condos, the owners often employ a manager
or a real estate company for this purpose. Some developers,
instead of relinquishing control, keep a finger in the pie
through hidden ownership in a real estate firm which obtains
a long-term management contract. Such arrangements may result in high fees and poor service.

If you are buying a condo on resale, the seller will tell you
who runs the development. You should check with other
condo owners to determine the performance of the managers.
If you are buying a new unit, find out if the developer plans to
be involved with the management of the condo. In either case,
as an owner, be prepared to attend association meetings and
possibly to run for election to the association board.

The association may have certain powers over resale, particularly in the case of cooperatives. For example, the association must approve of new buyers before a resale can be con-

cluded. If you wish to sell, your transaction could be impeded by an association veto of your buyer.

Check list on buying a condo or co-op

If you are planning to purchase a condo or co-op, consider whether your unit or shares will appreciate in value and what effect rising costs and factors such as a building mortgage will have on your interests.

The present condition of the building or complex is a guide to the future costs you will share through increased maintenance charges or other assessments.

For example, the maintenance charges presented at first may seem reasonable and affordable. But, sometimes in a new condo, a developer may hold maintenance charges down until the units are sold. After he has left, the owners find mounting costs make higher monthly assessments necessary. Local officials may be able to advise you about reasonable charges. If you are buying on resale, ascertain if major expensive repairs can be predicted. They will lead to subsequent increases in the monthly assessment.

The present condition of the building or complex is a guide to the future costs you will share through increased maintenance charges or other assessments. Know how much cash is in the building's reserve fund to meet heavy repairs or new installations of equipment. A low reserve means that owners may be subject to cost-covering charges. The state of the plumbing and wiring is crucial, as is the condition of the roof and boiler. Observe any shoddiness, unfinished areas, and mere cosmetic improvements. If you live in a building complex undergoing conversion, a tenants' engineer should inspect the buildings and make an assessment. As an outsider, you may need to hire a home inspector versed in the condo/co-op market to give you a report.

The model apartment you may be shown in a new development or a conversion may not be representative of other units.

To help you make a realistic judgment, try to meet residents of finished units or present tenants in a conversion situation.

Your lawyer will examine all documents, advise you of your present rights, future difficulties that might develop, and whether the underlying mortgage for the building will fall due and affect you now or complicate a later resale. Since the laws are highly technical and the field is changing rapidly, your advisor should be a specialist in the condo/co-op area. Do not sign anything without specific advice from your attorney.

Prior to consulting an attorney, you can make your own investigations and comparisons. A guide, "Questions About Condominiums," is free from the Consumer Information Center, Pueblo, CO 81009. This publication of the U.S. Department of Housing and Urban Development offers helpful pointers on many of the legal complexities of condo ownership.

If you are considering a new condo, investigate the reputation of the developer. Call the local Better Business Bureau; contact the state's real estate commission and the office of the attorney-general; if necessary, get in touch with the U.S. Department of Consumer Affairs in Washington, D.C. An area office of the Department of Housing and Urban Development (HUD) may be able to give you background information. Also, find out if your down payment is protected. Your deposit should be placed in a separate escrow account. If you allow your funds to be co-mingled with those of the developer, and he fails to sell all the units or leaves the development partially built, your down payment may be lost.

Acquaint yourself with your rights under state or federal law. Some states have lagged in protecting condo buyers against abuses. In New York, state law is tight. In Florida, where condo growth was and continues to be particularly heavy, new law was slow to catch up with buyer need; it is now improving. Tenant protection provided by local laws on conversion of apartments to condominium or cooperative ownership must be investigated. There are widespread differences not only across the country but even within a county.

In new condos, you must check out everything the salesperson promised. Plans for the condo should be on file with the county clerk. Developers and their salespeople may play down local real estate taxes, promise recreational areas and fail to supply them, or underestimate closing costs. You may be told you have ownership and free use of garage space, the pool, the tennis courts, or other recreational facilities, while in fact the developer has retained rights that compel you to pay "rent" for their use. Finally, determine whether the developer controls the utilities. If this is so, rates may zoom or there may be inadequate service, and the owners lack redress.

In a resale, ask the seller to show you the master deed and the rules regarding children, pets, guests, and renting out your unit. This information will help you determine if the condo fits your lifestyle.

Other considerations. Can you afford to buy? When interest rates are high and mortgages or loans hard to obtain, some people miscalculate costs. In a condo/co-op situation, you may be misled by apparently reasonable maintenance costs. Also, check into the operating budget, as well as repair projections.

Can you rent your unit to a tenant if the need arises? A single-family home may be rented while the owners await a suitable buyer or price, but rules at a condominium or co-operative may deny or limit that option. While it is desirable to screen out renters who might not maintain the unit suitably, you should consider how the rules might affect you adversely.

Is the property a conversion? An old building converted to condo or co-op status requires detailed checking. If you are a tenant, you may know better than to buy—having seen the report of the tenant group's engineer who projects heavy repairs and finds negative factors, such as termite infestation and substandard electrical wiring. As an outsider, you may be charmed by the model apartment and cosmetic improvements, but talking to longtime tenants may inform you of incurable plumbing problems and the ineffectiveness of the improvements with which a salesperson has impressed you. If a majority of tenants is fighting the conversion, you may suspect that over the years the property may entail more financial burden than profit.

Can you resell easily? Not only must you examine the internal conditions of the property, but you must consider the area in general as well. Its location, the character of the neighborhood, and access to business and shopping areas, schools and churches, as well as other facilities, will affect chances of resale, particularly during difficult economic periods. Any restrictions placed on resale by an owners' association may weigh negatively in some otherwise desirable situations.

Chapter 8

YOUR LIFE INSURANCE PROGRAM

YOUR financial responsibilities to your dependents will dictate your life insurance coverage. If you are single, or married and working with no dependents, you do not need life insurance, though you may want it to provide funds to a beneficiary at death. If you have dependents, life insurance is a necessary expense which should be included in your budget.

The purpose of this chapter is to help you estimate the amount of insurance you need and to explain the types of policies now available.

How much insurance do you need?

You cannot know exactly how much insurance your family will need since the date of your death is unknown. However, you can try to make an estimate by using your current financial status and family requirements as a guide.

Consider the expenses your family would face at your death: funeral costs and possibly medical bills for a final illness, mortgage payments, and living expenses for your surviving spouse and children or other dependents. The amount required for living expenses will vary, depending on whether your spouse works and the number of years the children or other dependents will require support and education.

> **. . . it will generally require at least 75% of your monthly after-tax income in insurance coverage to maintain your family's current standard of living.**

Add the approximate cost of these financial needs and compare this figure with the estimated benefits to be paid by Social Security and such sources as employee benefits, and estimated income from sources within the dependents' control. If there is a deficit, life insurance has to cover it.

Excluding items like college expenses, it will generally require at least 75% of your monthly after-tax income in insurance coverage to maintain your family's current standard of living. One insurance company states that to provide each $100 of monthly income for ten years, $8,500 in life insurance or other income-producing assets will be needed. Thus if your monthly net after-tax income is $3,000, you want to provide $2,250 (75% of $3,000) each month. To do this, you will need 22.5 times $8,500 or $191,250 worth of insurance to provide $2,250 a month for ten years.

To estimate your insurance needs, follow these steps:

STEPS	FILL-IN	EXAMPLE
1. 75% of your annual after-tax pay	$ _____	$30,000
2. Less: Social Security benefits payable to your dependents annually	_____	5,000
3. Shortfall	_____	25,000
4. Divide shortfall by interest currently payable. For example, if 10% is currently payable, divide the shortfall by .10	_____	250,000
5. Less: Total of your savings	_____	50,000
6. This is the amount of capital your family needs and may be provided by insurance	$ _____	200,000

The sum of the savings plus insurance earning interest at the rate estimated, in addition to Social Security benefits, will return annually to your dependents an amount equal to 75% of your annual after-tax income. This rule of thumb must be adjusted for your situation. If you are carrying debts that your dependents would have to pay or if you wish to provide for additional funds for a child's college education, more coverage would be required. If your spouse works or if your dependents have other sources of income, it may not be necessary to replace 75% of your after-tax income.

As your family or economic conditions change, you should review your insurance coverage and project your family's needs from the new vantage point.

Naming beneficiaries

You intend your life insurance proceeds to benefit those financially dependent on you, in most cases your spouse and children, but sometimes your parents. Be sure you name them correctly as owners and/or beneficiaries of your policies to avoid later problems.

When you take out a policy, reserve the right to change the beneficiaries. If you do not make this proviso, you must have written consent from the formerly named beneficiary before the insurance company will make the change. The situation might become particularly involved in case of divorce. Perhaps, after a financial settlement has been reached, a former spouse should not benefit from a policy already in force. A change of beneficiaries would have to be made.

Your insurance company has a legal staff, and if your personal situation is complicated, you should have your agent refer the case to these lawyers.

If you are consulting an attorney about your will and estate planning, discuss the question of insurance with him or her. As the years bring changes, you will undoubtedly find that you must alter the names or the order of your life insurance beneficiaries.

Term insurance

The first type of policy to consider is term insurance. Term insurance is pure protection for as long as premiums are paid;

there is no cash value buildup as there is with whole-life insurance. For lowest rates on term insurance, you should look to group policies offered by your employer, an association you

---

Since your purpose in acquiring life insurance usually is to provide death benefits for your dependents' support or to provide liquidity for your estate, term insurance offers the largest benefits for the lowest cost.

---

belong to, or if you live in a state which allows such plans, savings bank insurance.

Despite insurance agents' sales pitches that whole life is the better form of life insurance, term insurance is preferable in almost every instance. Since your purpose in acquiring life insurance usually is to provide death benefits for your dependents' support or to provide liquidity for your estate, term insurance offers the largest benefits for the lowest cost. For example, coverage equal to one year's earnings for a man aged 35 takes 1.65% of his gross annual earnings if he buys a whole-life policy, compared with 0.32% for a term policy. In dollars, a man earning $75,000 annually will pay $1,238 for a whole-life policy, but only $240 for the same coverage under a term policy.

The cost of term insurance is easy to determine. Premium costs are listed for age and face amount. You pay slightly more if premiums are to be paid other than annually. You merely have to compare the premium rates offered by different insurers. Term insurance offers coverage for a specific span of time, covering either a certain number of years, often one, two, or five years, or up to a certain age. Usually, term policies do not go beyond age 70.

Cost should not be the only criterion in selecting a policy. Check on your right to renew in case of disability and options to convert to whole-life insurance. A conversion option allows you to convert without giving evidence of insurability. However, you may have to inform the company that you intend to convert, and the policy may have a deadline for doing so. For instance, if you have a ten-year term policy, you may have to announce your intention to convert before the first seven years have elapsed.

Renewable term insurance is preferable because renewal rates are stated and guaranteed, even though rates may rise in the meantime. In addition, you do not have to produce evidence of insurability when you renew your policy. Even if your health fails, you can still renew.

Term insurance may be used in addition to whole-life insurance when you have extra risks to cover at certain times. Also, a decreasing term policy may help your spouse meet a mortgage debt in case of your death. As the amount of debt and the consequent financial responsibility decrease, so does the amount of coverage.

Deposit term insurance. Like a regular term policy, deposit term insurance covers you for a ten-year period and is renewable. However, in the first year you pay a deposit in addition to the annual premium—typically $10 per $1,000 of coverage. For example, a $75,000 policy would require a deposit of $750. At the end of the ten years, the deposit plus interest is returned. However, you may forfeit your deposit if you drop the policy. While deposit term insurance is so recent that consumer groups have yet to evaluate it fully, it is probably true that you could get a better return on your deposit by investing that money elsewhere.

Whole-life insurance

With whole-life insurance (also referred to as straight life, ordinary life, or permanent insurance), you pay a fixed premium; you receive life coverage and other stated benefits. Your age when you buy the policy fixes the premium rate that you will continue to pay. Your policy acquires a "cash value" because the company invests part of the premiums. As the cash surrender values increase, the element of pure insurance decreases. The cash value does not increase the face amount of the policy. However, it may be useful in raising loans and can help you to cover the cost of your insurance if, at some time, you are unable to pay premiums.

The disadvantage of whole-life policies is the low return on the amount invested. In recent years, consumers have realized the poor investment feature of whole life, and some insurance companies no longer offer it. While whole-life policies have been touted as "forced savings vehicles," you would probably do better to invest the money elsewhere. You do have access to your "savings," but at a price; you pay the insurance company interest to withdraw your equity.

There is one advantage to whole life that may make sense for those in top tax brackets: the tax-shelter aspect of dividends on whole-life policies. Dividends are tax free because the IRS views them as a refund of premiums. If you allow the dividends to accumulate, the company reinvests them, producing a greater benefit. At death, they pass tax free to the beneficiary.

The disadvantage of whole-life policies is the low return on the amount invested.

On a whole-life policy, you may discontinue premium payments and choose one of the following options: you can receive less insurance protection throughout your life (based on the cash value); you can set an ending date to the full protection; you can obtain a cash settlement for your canceled policy; or instead of life insurance, you may elect to receive income for a certain period.

Your policy will automatically put one of these provisions into effect if you fail to pay premiums. Check to find out which it will be because, if you cannot pay, you may wish to arrange for a different provision to be made.

Limited-payment life. This policy is actually straight life, but with premiums payable within a stated time, say 20 or 30 years, or by a certain age, such as 65, instead of being payable annually over a lifetime. The higher premiums build up cash values faster, but the cost might prove burdensome to a young person who generally does not reach highest earning capacity until mid-life. For the person whose early years mark the high earning point (an athlete or model, for example), a limited-payment policy may prove desirable.

Endowment policies. These policies, like limited-payment life policies, are written for a certain number of years or until a specified age. The buyer is insured for those years and will receive a stated amount when the policy falls due. If the buyer does not live to collect, the beneficiary receives the face amount of the policy.

If the buyer fails to keep up the premiums, there is a penalty and only part of the investment, plus dividends, can be recovered. Endowment policies also include the main features of straight life insurance, such as availability for loans and surrender value. However, they are poor insurance choices for most people because they do not provide the greatest insurance protection and are extremely expensive.

Combination policies and other new types of insurance

As discussed above, insurance companies offer many types of policies, varying premium payments and coverage at different ages. A policy may combine permanent with term options. Another policy may offer substantial coverage during the period the insured has young children, with a decrease in coverage afterward. Another policy may start with low premiums followed by an increase that will level out after a period of time. To meet competition and changing economic conditions, insurance companies have found it profitable and even necessary to introduce variations and combinations of basic insurance policies. You may want a policy with flexible options, but before buying, check the policy for the return paid on your investment. If it is low, the policy may not be suitable since low investment return actually increases the cost of the policy.

Universal life. A relatively new option in life insurance is universal life, which was introduced by E. F. Hutton Life Insurance Company in 1979. It is basically a renewable term policy with a premium that changes annually, combined with a cash value account. The premiums go into a fund, part of which pays for insurance coverage and the other part is invested.

The attractiveness of universal life is its flexibility and higher earnings. The policyholder decides the schedule for payment of premiums and may also change the face value of the policy. If cash is withdrawn from the policy, it is not considered a loan; the individual does not have to repay principal or interest, though the company may charge a small fee. If the policyholder skips some premium payments, the cash account will be used to cover them. Interest is paid on the cash value based on the company's investments or on a given index, such as Treasury securities, and there is usually a guaranteed minimum return, often 4%. These rates are higher than the traditionally low return on whole-life policies. During a period of high interest rates, universal life is appealing. Withdrawals are taxed to the extent that the cash value exceeds the investment in the contract. There are also penalties for premature withdrawals. Be cautioned that the proceeds of a universal life policy are tax free to beneficiaries only if the policy meets certain tests spelled out in the law.

Universal-life policyholders receive a statement each year disclosing the current amount of insurance and cash value, as well as the current interest rate on their investment. Policyholders are also given a breakdown of how much of their money is going to insurance, to investments, and to company fees.

The attractiveness of universal life is its flexibility and higher earnings.

It should be noted that actual return on investment of universal-life policies does not equal the high advertised rates because fees reduce the policyholder's earnings in the first few years. Further, future returns are dependent on market rates, which fluctuate.

Universal life currently requires a substantial amount of coverage, often a minimum of $100,000 and higher. It is now offered only in some states, and many of the large insurance companies do not sell it.

Adjustable life. This type of policy preceded universal life but is not as widely offered. It allows flexibility in insurance coverage since you may change the term, amount of coverage, premium payment periods, and even type of policy, such as switching from term to whole life. However, this policy does not offer the higher yield of universal life.

Variable life. This policy, like universal life, is income oriented. It has fixed premiums and a guaranteed minimum death benefit, but no minimum guaranteed cash value. Part of your premium covers insurance costs and part is invested in a mutual fund offered by the insurance company.

Your return depends on the performance of the mutual fund. Since this policy is considered a securities investment, it must be registered with the Securities and Exchange Commission and offer a prospectus.

Joint life. Two new types of policies designed for working couples are joint life insurance and survivorship joint life insurance. Currently, only a limited number of companies offer them.

Joint life insurance pays benefits only on the death of the first spouse to die. The surviving spouse must then seek individual coverage. Premiums for a joint life policy are higher than for a similar individual policy on the life of one spouse, but less expensive than paying for two individual policies. Joint life is available as a whole life, a level term, or a decreasing term policy. Whether a joint life policy is the best choice for a couple depends on their financial needs. If both spouses earn substantial incomes and each could be self-supporting in the event of the other's death, joint life may be the right coverage. It could provide the proceeds necessary to pay a single large expense, like college for a child or paying off the mortgage.

In contrast to joint life, a survivorship joint life policy pays benefits only after the death of the second spouse. This policy is designed chiefly to pay estate taxes of the second estate. In the aftermath of the new tax law, survivorship joint life may become popular since, as a result of the new unlimited marital deduction, there may be no estate tax due on the estate of the first spouse to die. However, the estate of the second spouse to die may have an increased tax burden due to the inclusion in the second estate of all the marital deduction property.

Family income. With a separate policy or rider, you may obtain term insurance plus a guaranteed monthly income for your dependents for a certain period. If you die during that period, your beneficiary receives a monthly income from the date of your death. If you survive the stated period, the policy pays nothing.

Say your wife is the beneficiary. Depending on the company issuing the policy, there will be a choice of ways in which she could benefit. She might receive your basic policy's benefits immediately with monthly income until the end of the period of coverage. She could reserve payment of the main benefit until after the monthly payments run out. She could split the main benefit, receiving a portion when the monthly payments start and the rest when they end.

The appeal of a family income policy is greatest for a husband concerned that, on his premature death, he would be survived by a young widow with minor children. Such a policy combines permanent insurance with decreasing term coverage. It can provide an extra in the form of monthly income which starts on the death of the insured and continues for a specified period, for example, 15 or 20 years from the date the policy was originally purchased. Monthly income is a percentage of the insurance coverage, such as 1% per $1,000 ($10) permanent insurance. At the end of the monthly income period, the face amount of permanent insurance is paid to the beneficiary. Note that monthly income is paid only if the insured dies prematurely within the specified period. For instance, assume a man buys a $50,000, 20-year family income policy, paying $500 monthly income (1% of $50,000 face). If he dies one year after purchase, his beneficiary would get $500 a month for 19 years and then the $50,000 face amount. On the other hand, if he lives for 21 years after purchasing the policy, his beneficiary would not get any monthly income, but would receive an immediate payment of $50,000.

Family maintenance. This policy is a combination of permanent insurance and level term insurance. Unlike the family income policy, the period over which monthly income payments will be made to the beneficiary starts at the time of the insured's death, if he dies within a specified period. For instance, a husband, 30 years old, buys a 20-year, 1% family maintenance policy, $25,000 face. If he dies prior to age 50, his widow-beneficiary will receive $250 a month for a full

20 years and then payment of $25,000. However, if he dies after age 50, there will be no monthly income payments, but the $25,000 face amount will be paid immediately to the widow.

A portion of each monthly income payment will reflect interest return on the permanent insurance part of the policy left on deposit. This interest is taxable income to the beneficiary. The remaining portion of each monthly payment will reflect an installment settlement of term coverage, constituting principal (tax free) and interest return. The interest portion, though, can be freed from tax—up to $1,000 a year—if the surviving spouse is the beneficiary. The lump-sum payment made when monthly income ceases is tax-free income.

Family plan. A family plan policy is combined permanent and term insurance covering all members of the family. This is how the policy operates: The father is the primary insured, covered by permanent insurance in the largest amount. His wife and minor children are secondary insureds, covered by term insurance in smaller amounts. While it is true that secondary beneficiaries normally survive the primary beneficiary, premature deaths do occur. Although insurance recovery on the death of a secondary beneficiary is comparatively small, it may provide the funds needed to meet bills resulting from the dependent's last illness or funeral costs. Or if the mother of the family dies, funds are available for child care while adjustments are made to new conditions.

Insurance on wife and children is offered by some companies as a rider to the husband's insurance.

Check to see if your company issues this type of life insurance. A common package would be $50,000 whole-life protection for the father, and term coverage of $10,000 each on the lives of the mother and children. Variations of the family plan are favorites with insurance agents who sell them, but do not necessarily offer worthwhile protection in many situations.

Riders

When you buy a life insurance policy, you will be offered additional benefits, usually at prices lower than if they were bought separately. Among the more common riders are:

Guaranteed insurability. This provision allows you to buy additional insurance at specified times to a stated age limit without having to prove insurability.

Accidental death. In case of death because of an accident which is stated by the rider (illness is not included), the amount of the policy is doubled or tripled. This rider is good only up to age 60 or 65.

Waiver disability. If you become totally disabled before age 60 or 65, the company will pay your premiums and thus continue your insurance. Another disability rider provides a monthly payment equal to 1% of the face amount of your policy if you are totally disabled.

Cost-of-living adjustment. This provision allows you to increase your coverage at stated periods so your insurance keeps pace with inflation. You do not have to prove insurability for these increases.

Separate policies for children

Your insurance agent or your children's school may try to interest you in separate life insurance policies for your children. Generally, these policies are an unnecessary expense. First, the risk of death during childhood is extremely low. Second, if a death did occur, most families would be able to bear the cost of burial. If this cost would be a problem, a rider attached to the parents' policy to cover the expense would be less expensive than a separate policy. You may be tempted by the low premiums offered, but you and your children would gain more by putting the same amount into a savings account or other investment.

One argument in favor of policies for children is that they continue until age 21 and the child can then take over payments for an adult policy. However, most young, healthy adults will have no problem getting insurance.

Grandparents sometimes buy policies as gifts to children. Again, the money would be put to better use in a savings account or other investment.

Know your insurance agent

Although savings bank life insurance is available in certain states directly from banks, the bulk of life insurance is sold by agents who are sometimes employees of a company and may or may not receive a salary in addition to commission. Usually, agents are self-employed and work only on a commission basis. (Bear this factor in mind and ask yourself if the

---

Remember, you rely on your agent not only to recommend one insurance policy, but to periodically review and update your coverage.

---

agent is advising you to buy protection your family requires, or if it just pays a higher commission.)

When you consider the great importance of life insurance to your family's security and the amount of money you will invest, you should be fully satisfied with the agent who will be making far-reaching recommendations to you. Remember, you rely on your agent not only to recommend one insurance policy, but to periodically review and update your coverage. If the agent uses "C.L.U." after his or her name, you are assured the agent is a Chartered Life Underwriter and has successfully completed examinations and other requirements set by the American College of Life Underwriters.

Discounts

Check with your agent for any discounts you may be eligible to receive. For example, some companies reduce the cost of policies for nonsmokers. Also, some companies are eliminating the higher premiums charged to policyholders who are considered risks because of a heart ailment or other disease. Or your company may give discounts to policyholders who follow a preventive health care routine, for example, those who exercise regularly by jogging.

Mail-order insurance

You may be attracted by an advertisement in which an insurance company in a distant state offers life (or other) insurance. Responding to the advertisement may bring a salesperson to your doorstep. Because of the distance, you will have little or no chance of checking on the reliability of the company. Maybe it is sound, maybe the salesperson can give good advice, but it is wiser to do business near home and on a direct basis. Also, you run the risk that the distant company is not licensed to sell in your state. You lose out on the protection your state law may provide, and perhaps open the door to legal complications at your death.

Canceling or switching existing policies

If a policy is no longer needed, you should cancel it; whether you should switch policies depends on any savings to be made by dropping the old policy for the new one. All things being equal, new insurance will cost you more than the same insurance bought when you were younger. However, in some cases, a switch may provide a saving where the old policy pays no dividends but the new policy does. A switch should not be made unless a careful review of net premium costs is made in relation to dividend payments and investment return. Further, proceed with caution if the switch has been touted by an agent who wants you to drop some other company's policy to take his or hers. Only if careful investigation proves that the agent had a valid point should you let a former policy lapse in favor of a new one.

Your employer may help buy your insurance coverage

Your company may be able to help you obtain additional protection through a split-dollar insurance plan. Under this plan, your employer purchases permanent life insurance on your life and pays the annual premium to the extent of the yearly increases in the cash surrender value of the policy; you pay only the balance of the premium. At your death, your employer is entitled to part of the proceeds equal to the cash surrender value or any lesser amount equaling the total premiums paid. You have the right to name a beneficiary to receive the remaining proceeds which, under most policies, are substantial compared to the employer's share.

You report annually as taxable income an amount equal

to the one-year term cost of the declining life insurance protection to which you are entitled less any portion of the premium provided by you. Simplified somewhat, here is how the tax would be figured in one year. Assume the share of the proceeds payable to your beneficiary (face value less cash surrender value) from a $100,000 policy is $77,535. If the term cost of $77,535 insurance provided by the employer is $567, you pay tax on $567, less your payment of premium. If you paid a premium of $209, you pay tax on $358 ($567 − $209). Assume in the fourth year you pay no premium and the amount payable to your family is $69,625. (Under the split-dollar plan, the benefits payable to your beneficiary decline continuously; the employer's share increases annually because of the continued payment of premiums and the increase in the cash surrender value.) The term cost provided by your employer toward $69,625 is $549; you pay tax on the full $549.

Despite the tax cost, you may find the arrangement an inexpensive method of obtaining additional insurance coverage with your employer's help. For example, taking the taxable premium benefit of $549 from the above example, if you are in the 32% bracket, the cost of almost $70,000 insurance protection in that year is only $175.68 ($549 × 32%).

Group life

You may be able to participate in group life insurance coverage through your job, or as a member of a union, professional association, or some other group. You may have

---

Group insurance will rarely provide all the protection a family needs, but it can prove a useful addition to other policies and lower the overall cost of life insurance.

---

to contribute to the premium (some employers pay total cost), but your group term insurance will not cost as much as you would pay for an individual policy with similar coverage. Moreover, there may be no medical examination.

Usually, upon retirement or leaving a group, you can convert to individual whole life or endowment, but it will cost usual rates, which, if you were 65, would be extremely high. *Group paid up* is a plan which helps to overcome such undesirable features. Your contributions go toward paid-up whole-life insurance; your employer's go toward term, which covers your life. Upon retirement or leaving the group, you have your paid-up whole-life insurance which you can use in one of several ways. It can remain in force or be surrendered for cash or life income. You may also be able to buy additional whole-life insurance which will make up for what your employer formerly paid in term coverage.

Group insurance will rarely provide all the protection a family needs, but it can prove a useful addition to other policies and lower the overall cost of life insurance.

There is also a tax advantage to employer payments of group term insurance: premiums on up to $50,000 of coverage are tax-free fringe benefits.

In a state where savings bank insurance is available, your group may be able to take advantage of a plan offered to ten or more employees at low administrative cost.

Savings bank life insurance

If you live or work in a state where savings bank life insurance (SBLI) is sold, you have an excellent opportunity to obtain coverage at low rates. While state law limits the total amount of savings bank life insurance an individual may buy, a broad range of whole life, term endowments, and many variations can be obtained. All savings bank plans pay dividends, which further reduce the overall cost.

Age	5-YEAR RENEWABLE TERM		WHOLE LIFE	
	Male	Female	Male	Female
18	$ 66.90	$ 61.20	$ 247.80	$ 223.80
25	73.50	70.50	316.80	284.10
30	81.30	75.90	384.00	341.40
40	140.40	112.50	590.40	516.00
50	319.20	246.90	950.10	819.90
60	765.90	587.70	1,595.40	1,359.30

Above are sample premium rates for à $30,000 New York SBLI five-year renewable term policy and for a whole-life policy. Your age when you take out the policy will determine the rates.

At this writing, New York, Connecticut, and Massachusetts are the only states where the law permits savings bank life insurance. The rules of the system differ in the three states, but all offer SBLI to residents and those who work in the state. In New York, savings bank life insurance is available in amounts from $1,000 to $30,000. Maximums in Connecticut and Massachusetts are $15,000 and $53,000, respectively. Members of the immediate family—husband, wife, children, parents, brothers, and sisters—are also eligible. Connecticut savings banks also offer depositor's group term insurance to a maximum of $30,000.

Savings bank insurance is purchased directly from the bank; no agents are involved.

Veterans' insurance

On leaving the armed services, you should act to replace GI coverage within the 120-day period following discharge. An explanation of policy conversion rights issued by the Veterans Administration is provided for service personnel.

Veterans frequently fail to change the beneficiary's name in their National Service Life Insurance policy. Originally, their insurance may have been intended to benefit parents. If the veteran marries, a change of beneficiaries should be considered. Renaming beneficiaries of GI insurance is not complicated; consult your local Veterans' Service Agency.

The language of life insurance

Since the terms used in life insurance are not generally familiar, definitions of some are given below:

Beneficiary. The person named in the policy to receive the insurance money upon death of the insured.

Cash value. The money a policyholder can collect if the policy is canceled.

Convertible term insurance. Term insurance giving the insured the right to exchange the policy for permanent insurance without evidence of insurability.

Disability benefits. A rider which provides for either continuation of life insurance or a monthly benefit when the insured is proven totally and permanently disabled.

Dividend. Amount returned to participating policyholders as a refund of overpaid premiums. It is not taxable; but, being dependent on company operations, it is not guaranteed.

Endowment insurance. Payment of a definite sum to a policyholder, or his beneficiary, after a stated number of years.

Face amount. The sum stated on the face of the policy to be paid on death of the insured or at maturity.

Grace period. The period allowed after the premium due date for payment during which the policy does not lapse.

Insured. The person on whose life an insurance policy is issued.

Lapsed policy. A policy ended by nonpayment of premiums.

Limited-payment life insurance. Whole-life insurance paid for in a specified number of years.

Maturity. When the policy's face value is payable.

Nonparticipating policy. One that pays no dividends.

Ordinary life insurance. Also called straight life, it is payable by premiums until death.

Paid-up insurance. All premiums have been paid.

Participating policy. Dividends are payable.

Policy. The document in which the terms of the insurance contract are set forth and issued to the insured.

Policy loan. A loan made by the insurance company to a policyholder and secured by the cash value of his or her policy.

Premium. The regular periodic payment made for insurance.

Settlement options. Alternative ways in which the insured or beneficiary may have policy benefits paid.

Rider. An endorsement which changes the terms of an existing policy.

Term insurance. A policy payable at death if that event occurs during the term of the insurance.

Waiver of premium. A provision whereby an insurance company will keep a policy in force without payment of premiums. Usually operates as a disability benefit.

Whole-life insurance. Includes ordinary or straight life insurance on which premiums are payable until death and limited-payment life insurance on which premiums are paid for a certain number of years only.

Chapter 9
PERSONAL LIABILITY INSURANCE

FEW of us can afford the high cost of unexpected property losses and personal injuries or sickness. Personal security, if not peace of mind, necessitates the carrying of personal liability insurance. Insurance can replace home furnishings after a fire, pay damages if you are sued in a car accident, or cover doctor and hospital bills if you become ill or injured. The amount spent on premiums is often worth the security the insurance provides.

This chapter covers homeowner's and renter's insurance, automobile insurance, and health insurance.

Homeowner's and renter's insurance

A major decision for homeowners is not whether to carry insurance—most property owners do—but to make sure of adequate coverage. Sometimes underinsurance is caused by shortsighted efforts to cut corners, but more often by failure to take account of increases in the cost of replacing property. Construction costs, as well as many other property costs, have almost doubled in the last decade.

175

What can you do to make sure you are adequately insured? First, realistically appraise the value of your property and do so annually when your policy is up for renewal. See that your insurance coverage reflects changing values. Your insurance agent can advise you on the adequacy of your coverage. Experts advise policyholders to keep detailed inventories of their possessions. You can document items with photos, receipts, serial numbers, or records of appraisals. A written inventory should be kept in a safe deposit box or other safe place.

Second, consider adding to your policy an "inflation protection" clause which increases coverage and premiums automatically on your house and contents by a set percentage based on the construction cost index in your area.

Homeowner's policies are standardized. There are six standard homeowner's policies, generally described by the abbreviations HO–1, HO–2, HO–3, HO–4, HO–5, and HO–6. Four policies are for personal residences: HO–1, HO–2, HO–3, and HO–5; HO–6 is for condominium owners; HO–4 is for tenants. All cover common perils, such as fire, vandalism, glass breakage, and theft. They also offer comprehensive personal liability coverage in case someone is injured accidentally in or around your home, and they provide for limited medical payments. The recommended amount of liability coverage is $100,000. High-income homeowners may be more vulnerable to claims and should consider separate personal liability coverage (discussed below).

HO–1 is the basic policy for homeowners, while HO–5 is the most comprehensive. Ask your agent for a brochure which describes the protection features and exclusions of each. Compare, ask for advice, and then decide whether the wider coverage policy is worth the added cost.

When you have decided which type of policy to buy, check the premium rates by calling several insurance companies. Premiums vary because insurance costs are determined by each company's past experience in the area, the construction of your house, whether it is supplied by city water or a well, its closeness to a fire hydrant, and other factors.

If you decide to buy more extensive and expensive coverage, you may reduce insurance cost by raising the amount of the "deductible," the amount you pay out-of-pocket before insurance takes over. As much as 10% may be saved on your annual premium if you increase the deductible from $100 to $250. A $500 deductible might produce a 20% saving.

On any policy, you are insured only for the perils listed, and there are limits on coverage of selected personal property. Examples of such limits are: $100 for money, bullion, gold other than goldware, silver other than silverware, platinum, coins, and medals; $500 for securities, deeds, manuscripts, tickets, and passports; $500 for theft of jewelry, watches, furs, and precious and semiprecious stones; $1,000 for theft of silverware, goldware, and pewterware. Also, regular policies may not cover some items, such as antiques or fine art.

If coverage is limited or nonexistent on a regular policy, you may buy a floater policy to insure these items.

On any policy, you are insured only for the perils listed, and there are limits on coverage of selected personal property.

How much insurance should you carry? The land and foundation of your house are not insurable, and in figuring insurable value, an average 20% of the value of the house is generally allocated to land, 5% to the foundation. This leaves 75% of value to the house. To allow for full coverage of losses in case of partial damage to your house, you have to insure up to 80% of the value of the house. Coverage of less than 80% means that you become a co-insurer of your home. Here is how co-insurance works: If the value of your house (not including land and foundation) is $75,000, you should insure the house for at least $60,000 (80% of $75,000). If you insure for $30,000 and suffer damage of $5,000, the company would pay only half of the damage. This is because you are deemed to be the insurer of half the loss as you only owned half the required coverage. However, even where you meet the 80% test, recovery for a total loss is limited to the face amount of your policy. To protect for a total loss of your property, the face amount would have to cover 100% of the value of the house.

Policies are usually written to cover the contents of a house for up to 50% of the amount of the coverage on the house itself. You may be able to buy a policy endorsement to increase this coverage to 70% of the coverage on the house. As mentioned above, you may wish to use a floater to insure particular items.

Note that standard policies pay only the depreciated cost of damaged or stolen personal property. You may upgrade your coverage by buying replacement-value insurance. Under a replacement-value policy you would be reimbursed for the cost of buying substantially equal property. Such coverage costs about 10% more (e.g., a $600 standard policy could be upgraded to replacement value coverage for about $60 more).

Personal umbrella policy. To supplement your homeowner's liability insurance coverage, you may consider an umbrella policy. The umbrella coverage takes over where the homeowner's policy leaves off. Coverage usually runs from $1 million and higher and is recommended mainly for wealthy individuals whose assets may be exposed in a liability suit. The cost of such coverage is minimal; $2 million protection can be bought for less than $100 a year.

When you cannot get a regular homeowner's policy, typically in high-crime areas, you may be able to buy federal crime insurance or insurance through a state program. The insurance covers burglary, robbery, damage to your home during an actual or attempted theft, and theft from a locked car trunk. Premiums vary with location. To get this type of insurance, you must install certain locks on doors and windows.

Your state may also participate in the Fair Access to Insurance Requirements (FAIR) programs. These are insurance company pooling arrangements to provide insurance to homeowners who cannot obtain a regular policy.

For details on programs available in your state, write to your state insurance department.

Flood insurance. Flood insurance may be available under a government-subsidized National Flood Insurance Program (NFIP). NFIP coverage is offered by the Department of Housing and Urban Development (HUD) for areas that have undertaken flood-control protection. The amount of available insurance depends on the rating given to your area. When a community first qualifies under the NFIP program it is in emergency status, and during that time you can buy up to $35,000 of flood insurance on a single-family dwelling and coverage for the contents of your house up to $10,000. After premium rates are set in your area, emergency status ends and you may then buy up to $185,000 of coverage on your house and $60,000 on the contents. All types of buildings, including commercial, may be insured under the program.

Generally, employers are liable for medical benefits and lost wages when a worker is injured on the job or becomes ill from job-related causes, but only in recent years have workers' compensation laws been extended to include household workers.

Discounts. Some insurance companies give discounts on policies to homeowners who have installed fire and burglar alarms. Ask your insurance agent whether your company offers these discounts.

Insurance for household employees. If you employ household workers, such as a babysitter or maid or gardener, you may need more coverage than your standard homeowner's policy provides. Twenty-four states require homeowners to provide insurance against injury to household workers. Generally, employers are liable for medical benefits and lost wages when a worker is injured on the job or becomes ill from job-related causes, but only in recent years have workers' compensation laws been extended to include household workers. Independent contractors, such as repairmen who have many customers, are excluded from this group in many states. Laws determining when a worker must be covered are different in each state. Check with your insurance agent or lawyer to find out whether you need additional coverage.

Auto insurance

Auto insurance is required by law in many states; in others you do not have to buy it until your first accident. Nevertheless, you should carry liability insurance to protect yourself in case you are ever in an accident.

When shopping for auto insurance, first decide what coverage you need and then call a few insurance companies. Ask your friends what companies they use and check the annual *Consumer Reports Buying Guide* (December issue) for ratings of customer satisfaction with various insurance companies.

Types of coverage. Auto insurance policies offer different kinds of coverage to pay for injuries to you and your passengers or injuries caused by you, and to pay for property damage. Here are the types of coverage available:

Liability insurance pays for two kinds of damages. Bodily injury liability protects you if you injure someone; property damage liability pays for damage to another person's car or other property. The amount of insurance is usually abbreviated as a set of three numbers, for example, 100/300/25. The numbers represent thousands of dollars. The first number, $100,000, represents the maximum amount the company would pay in case of injury to or death of one person. The second number, $300,000, represents the maximum amount the company would pay in the injury to or death of two or more persons. The last number, $25,000, is the maximum amount payable for property damage.

Many states require 10/20/5 as a minimum amount of insurance. However, experts recommend buying 100/300/25 since damage awards are often very high. Those with high incomes or substantial assets should consider greater coverage.

If your car is a few years old and not very valuable, collision coverage is probably unnecessary. The insurance company would pay only the car's cash value.

In states where no-fault insurance is sold, each driver's insurance pays his or her injury claim up to the policy limit. However, substantial liability coverage is still recommended since the driver at fault can be sued if the claim surpasses a level set by state law. These levels are generally low. Also, a driver may be liable when driving in a state that does not have no-fault insurance.

Collision insurance covers damage to your car. It is usually bought for new cars. If your car is a few years old and not very valuable, collision coverage is probably unnecessary. The insurance company would pay only the car's cash value. However, if you have taken out a loan to buy a car, consider collision insurance since you will be paying for the car over a long period of time, even if it is damaged or destroyed in an accident. A lender may insist on collision coverage.

You can reduce the premiums for collision insurance by accepting a higher deductible, the amount you would pay out-of-pocket before insurance takes over.

If you do not carry collision coverage and have an accident, you may include a loss of more than $100 in your itemized deductions on your federal income tax return. The value of the deduction depends on your tax bracket.

Comprehensive insurance pays for damage other than by collision. This includes fire, vandalism, hail, flood, and theft. As with collision coverage, your car is insured for its cash value. An old car may not warrant the coverage. You may obtain fire and theft insurance alone at a lower cost than full comprehensive coverage.

Medical payments coverage pays medical expenses for you and your passengers whether or not an accident is your fault. Check the medical payments details carefully as they will vary. Some policies do not pay for items covered by your regular health insurance policy. Some will pay for such things as eyeglasses and prescription drugs.

Uninsured motorist coverage protects you in case of injury to you or your passengers caused by an uninsured or hit-and-run driver. In some states this insurance is only for bodily injury while others also include property damage. Given the high number of uninsured drivers on the road, this coverage is worthwhile.

Wage loss and substitute services coverage is required in no-fault insurance states and optional in others. It replaces at least part of your wages if you are injured and provides for the cost of services you cannot perform as a result of your injury.

Premium rates. How much you pay for auto insurance will depend on the coverage and the company you choose. Other factors which affect your premiums are:

1. Age—young drivers, from age 17 through 25, are considered a high risk, and thus pay more.
2. Sex—young men are considered a greater risk than young women. However, in some states, age and sex may not be used in determining risk.
3. Marital status—young married people usually pay less than young single men. Some companies consider divorced or widowed persons a high-risk group.
4. Driving record—someone who has been involved in an accident or has received speeding tickets will pay more than an individual who has a clean driving record. A good record for a minimum period, often three years or five years, or completion of a driver's education course, may also entitle you to discounts.
5. Use—whether the car is used infrequently for leisure activities or daily for commuting to work or for business. Also, the number of drivers using the car affects the premium.
6. Location—insuring a car in an urban area costs more than in the suburbs or a small town. Within a city, there may be different premiums for different areas.
7. Occupation—insurance companies may classify some occupations as more risky than others.
8. Type and size of car—large cars cost more to insure than small cars. (The exception is a small sports car which costs more to insure.) Some insurance companies have begun to offer discounts on collision insurance for particular models which incur less damage in accidents and have lower repair costs than other cars in the same price range.

Health insurance

Health insurance is expensive; there are no bargain insurance rates, except for the lower rates of policies offered by group plans or employee plans of companies that provide health insurance as a tax-free fringe benefit. In planning your own purchase of health insurance, make sure you understand these terms.

Coverage. A policy describes the services paid for by insurance, for example, diagnostic x-rays, regular checkups, and listed surgical expenses. You should also read what the policy will not cover. Some usual exclusions are: diseases or physical impairments contracted before the policy was taken

---

All members of a family, not just the breadwinner, should be covered on a policy.

---

out (preexisting conditions); medical expense of care provided by a Veterans Administration hospital, state worker's compensation plan, or other federal or state programs; injuries received in a military action; pregnancies that began before the effective date of the policy; long-term care in a mental institution. Some policies now cover part or all of the cost of psychiatric treatment or consultation.

All members of a family, not just the breadwinner, should be covered on a policy. Children should be covered from the day of birth, though some policies do not begin coverage until 14 days after birth. Check your policy for details. Children may be automatically covered under a family plan; otherwise, you must notify the company and pay a higher premium to ensure coverage.

Children are usually covered on a parent's policy until age 19, or age 22 if they are full-time students. Find out when coverage lapses so you may immediately continue coverage for your child on an individual policy.

Spouses may be covered under the working spouse's group plan. Usually, this coverage ends 30 days after the death of the working spouse. Widows and widowers should then buy individual policies if they do not already have them.

Avoid buying specialized "dread diseases" policies. These cover only one or two serious diseases, for example, cancer. Maintaining adequate coverage with regular health insurance that includes all illnesses is better protection for your money.

Renewability. An optionally renewable or commercial policy may be renewed only if the company accepts your request for renewal. In addition, the company can change the premium rate on renewal. A guaranteed renewable policy is renewed at your election. The premium rate changes only if the company revises the rates for those in your classification. A noncancellable policy is a guaranteed policy that you can renew with no change in premium. For this privilege you are charged a higher premium at the outset. Paying the extra charge may be advisable if you are concerned about becoming seriously ill in the future, and thus becoming a poor insurance risk.

Blue Cross and Blue Shield insurance protection is generally renewable as long as you continue to pay premiums. (An older person wishing to supplement Medicare may have trouble *joining* the plan at a late date if he or she has a poor medical history.)

Method of payment. A benefit may be paid in terms of services or indemnity. In a service-type policy, the insurance organization pays for the service. For example, if the policy states that it will pay the cost of a semiprivate room, the type of payment is a service type. An indemnity policy will state that the insurance company will pay a stated sum per day for the cost of a hospital room. In general, room and board payments are based on the average rate most commonly charged for a semiprivate room and board in your area's hospitals. Consequently, premiums and payable rates will differ from city to suburb and across the country. When you choose a private room, a policy of this type would pay its stated semiprivate amount or the hospital's most common semiprivate room rate, if less; you pay the difference.

When you take out additional health insurance to back up your present coverage which is, say, group insurance at your place of employment, you will have to check carefully on the regulations governing the payment of benefits. Health associations and insurance companies are combining to ensure that there is no overpayment of benefits. Consequently, if your second, personal policy duplicates the benefits payable under your group policy, you may be paying premiums for benefits you cannot collect. The insuring agencies will settle the matter between themselves. Take care that you supplement, not duplicate, benefits.

Kinds of health insurance policies

The following types of insurance protection are available to offset these medical costs:

Hospitalization insurance. A hospital cost or hospitalization policy pays the cost of a hospital room and board for a number of days, and, generally, expenses such as drugs, operating room charges, and laboratory fees. The longer the hospitalization period covered, the more expensive the policy.

Some elective procedures may not be included in a hospitalization policy. Read the details of the policy. Some outpatient services may be covered in addition to hospitalization.

A major medical policy is tailored to protect you against severe rather than ordinary illness.

Surgical expense insurance. Here, the policy pays up to a specified amount for each type of operation or states that it will pay "reasonable" charges. X-rays and therapy may also be covered. The cost of a physician's visits in the hospital may be covered, but at an extra premium charge. Surgical insurance is often combined with a hospital cost policy.

Major medical insurance. This type of policy is generally taken out after you have coverage under a basic hospitalization-surgical policy. A major medical policy is tailored to protect you against severe rather than ordinary illness. This policy is considered necessary to pay the costs of a major illness.

Under a major medical policy, benefits are not paid until you or your basic hospital-surgical policy pays medical costs up to a stated deductible amount, usually from $100 to $1,000. Above the deductible, the policy pays 75% or 80% of costs up to a stated maximum. A maximum may be applied to each illness or to each member of a family. If there is a lifetime maximum applied to all the family and all illnesses, make sure it is a substantial sum. Some experts recommend a lifetime maximum of $250,000.

The other important figure to check on a major medical policy is the stop-loss limit. This is the annual limit of your share of costs. For example, say you have a major medical policy with a deductible of $200. After the deductible, the insurance company pays 80% of costs up to $5,000 and 100% of costs over $5,000. Thus the maximum you would pay on a bill of any size would be the $200 deductible plus 20% of $5,000 (since the company pays 80% of the first $5,000, you pay the remaining 20%) or $1,200. This amount is your stop-loss limit. Experts suggest that this amount be no more than 10% to 30% of your annual income.

Disability insurance. The above policies do not compensate you for income lost while you are ill. That is why disability insurance is so important, though it is often ignored. About 84 million people have some form of disability insurance, but only about one-quarter of this group has long-term coverage which pays benefits for a set number of years or to age 65.

Social Security includes disability insurance but only for severe disability. The strict requirements are:

1. Your condition must prevent you from doing any gainful work.
2. The disability must last at least 12 months or entail a condition expected to result in death.
3. Benefits do not begin until five months after applying.

A veteran may be eligible for a monthly benefit from veteran's insurance if the disability is service-related or if his income is below a specified level.

Worker's compensation provides disability payments; however, coverage varies from state to state.

Disability insurance may cover disability arising from an illness or an accident or both. Check the definition of disability in the policy you are considering. It should mean that you cannot work at your occupation. That you might find work in another occupation does not prevent you from collecting disability benefits. Payments are set at a monthly rate and usually begin after you have been disabled for a specified length of time. This is a point to consider carefully; premiums are lower if you do not begin to collect benefits right away, but your savings would have to cover the waiting period. Also, check whether partial disability is covered.

Rates for disability insurance vary. Large insurance companies usually sell disability policies, and some firms specialize in them.

Accidental death and dismemberment. This type of policy pays a set amount for death or injury caused by an accident. For example, the policy may pay $25,000 for accidental death and lesser amounts for severe injuries such as the loss of a hand.

Your life insurance policy may have provisions for disability or accidental death and dismemberment.

Medicare is discussed in Chapter 11.

Where to obtain health insurance

There are three sources of private medical and health insurance: (1) Blue Cross and Blue Shield insurance; (2) insurance companies; and (3) health maintenance organizations (HMOs) and other independent group practices, which may be organized by communities, unions, businesses, or insurance companies.

Blue Cross and Blue Shield. The protection offered by Blue Cross hospital and Blue Shield medical-surgical insurance will depend on location since the coverage and fees of these non-profit organizations vary from state to state. Be sure that your policy offers adequate coverage, or supplement your Blue Cross and Blue Shield coverage with additional insurance. Individuals and company groups sometimes combine basic Blue Cross hospital insurance with the comprehensive major medical plan of a commercial insurer.

Insurance companies. Commercial insurance comes in various forms, depending on whether it is geared to an individual or a group; to supplement other insurance such as Blue Cross; or to provide complete comprehensive coverage for a family. Comparison-shopping pays because of the differences in premiums, deductibles, and maximum coverage. Be careful with mail-order insurance. It may be confined to certain aspects of illness. In some cases, advertisements suggest generous benefits which are actually small when compared to hospital costs. Also, if a firm is not licensed to do business in your state, you will not be protected under your state's insurance laws in the event of a complaint against the company.

Health maintenance organizations. HMOs and similar groups are health care associations providing full medical services for a set fee each year. Some groups charge an additional small fee per visit. The HMOs often emphasize preventive health care and periodic examinations, which are rarely covered by conventional insurance. Usually, most services are available in one building or complex. You are required to use the doctors who belong to the group. Benefits vary at different HMOs, so compare plans before signing up.

Chapter 10

FINANCING A COLLEGE EDUCATION

A college education is no longer the sole right of the rich, but in today's economy, the rich may be the only ones who can easily afford a college education for their children. Students from families with limited funds may find the combination of high college costs and reduced federal aid a barrier to the quality education they would like to have.

Planning early and anticipating financial requirements is the best way to ensure an adequate higher education fund. Various saving vehicles are discussed later in this chapter.

. . . in today's economy, the rich may be the only ones who can easily afford a college education for their children.

However, most people put off dealing with the inevitable and, before they know it, their children are of college age. Here are ways to assess the financial requirements for a college education today and ways to satisfy those requirements.

How much does it cost?

When your child chooses a college, cost is only one factor in the decision; it should not be the most important one. Do not let high tuition rule out a college until you find out how much financial aid is available.

Living at home and attending a junior college or nearby college is the least expensive choice; living at your state university is the next. There, your child is eligible for state aid and, as a state resident, pays a lower rate than out-of-state students. Living at the university of another state is more expensive, but you still benefit from the generally lower tuition charged by state universities. The most expensive choice is to attend and live at a private college.

Do not let high tuition rule out a college until you find out how much financial aid is available.

When figuring expenses, keep in mind that tuition is not the only cost. Also include:

Fees—activity fees, breakage fees, room deposit fees, registration fees, and lab fees.
Books and supplies.
Room charges.
Meals and snacks.
Clothes and laundry.
Transportation—trips to and from home, plus local traveling.
Recreation and social activities.
Personal items—soap, shampoo, etc.
Telephone costs.

Sources of money for college

For most students, paying for college involves combining funds from work, financial aid, and family. Even at a prestigious institution such as Harvard University, 80% of the class of 1984 was receiving some financial aid in their freshman year. There are three kinds of financial aid: scholarships or grants, loans, and work-study programs.

Scholarships and grants do not have to be repaid. Scholarships may be awarded on the basis of academic achievement or other criteria. A student may have to maintain a certain grade-point average to renew the scholarships each year. Grants are usually awarded on the basis of financial need.

Check the following sources of scholarship money:

National Merit Scholarship Corporation—scholarships ranging from $250 to over $1,000 are awarded for one year or for up to four years. The awards are based on students' scores on the PSAT/NMSQT test taken in the junior year of high school.

If your child is involved in sports or has talent in music or art, he or she may be eligible for a scholarship on that basis.

State scholarships—some states offer scholarship money based on academic achievement. These scholarships usually have the restriction that they can only be used at a school located in the state.

Colleges—when your child has narrowed down the choice of schools, look into the types of scholarship each offers. They may have scholarships for academic achievement or for particular areas of study. If your child is involved in sports or has talent in music or art, he or she may be eligible for a scholarship on that basis. Ask whether these scholarships are automatically renewed for four years or are readjusted every year. Also, check local chapters of each school's alumni association for scholarships available.

High schools—scholarship money may be given to graduating seniors.

Labor unions and trade associations—college scholarships may be offered to children of members.

Corporations—scholarships may be available for children of employees.

Local civic and fraternal organizations—scholarships are often given to children of community residents. Check Elks, Lions, Rotary, Chamber of Commerce, Boys Club, and similar organizations.

ROTC—the Reserve Officers Training Corps awards scholarships to students who plan a career in the armed forces.

Churches and synagogues—scholarships may be given to children of members.

Federal grants, like most federal assistance, are based on need. A student's need is defined as the amount necessary for expenses after deducting the family's contribution. To be eligible for a federal grant, your child must be enrolled at least half time as a regular student in a qualified program at a participating school. Not every school participates in all federal assistance programs, so ask for information at financial aid offices of the schools being considered.

Pell Grants (formerly called Basic Educational Opportunity Grants) are for students from low-income families. Apply by filling out a Financial Aid Form (FAF) distributed by the College Scholarships Service, a Family Financial Statement (FFS) distributed by the American College Testing Program, or a U.S. Department of Education's Basic Grant Application Form. Four to six weeks later, the student receives a Student Eligibility Report (SER) which is notification of eligibility for a grant. The student must send a copy to the school he or she wishes to attend. The college's financial aid administrator completes the form and fills in the dollar amount of the award. For the 1981–1982 academic year awards ranged from $120 to $1,670. Pell Grants are automatically given when a student meets the requirements, and schools are not limited in the amount awarded.

Supplemental Education Opportunity Grants (SEOGs) are also for students from low-income families. These can be awarded in addition to Pell Grants. Students apply in the same way. Unlike Pell Grants, the Department of Education gives each school a set amount annually for SEOGs. These grants are awarded at the discretion of the school's financial aid administrator.

Veterans' benefits allow children of disabled or deceased veterans to receive up to $755 a year; ex-GIs can receive as much as $3,924 a year. For details on applying, contact the nearest office of the Veterans Administration.

State grants are awarded based on need. For information on your state's program, ask a high school guidance counselor.

Federal Guaranteed Student Loans are made through banks, but are guaranteed by the federal government. Also, the government pays the interest on the loan while the student is in school and contributes the difference between the low student rate and the market interest rate. For the 1981–1982 academic year, new students were paying 9% interest; students who already had loans and applied for another were paying 7%.

Students whose families have an adjusted gross income of up to $30,000 are automatically eligible. Families with higher incomes must prove need, and families whose adjusted gross income is $75,000 or more must meet a more stringent test. Students must pay an origination fee of 5% to defray the government's interest costs. The student does not have to begin repaying principal until 9 or 12 months after graduation and can stretch payments over ten years.

Undergraduate students can borrow up to $2,500 a year to a limit of $12,500 during undergraduate years. Graduate students can borrow up to $5,000 a year to a total of $25,000, including loans made while an undergraduate. In some states the maximums may be lower.

National Direct Student Loans are federally supported, low-interest loans made through the financial aid office of the school. Students should check with this office for the necessary forms. For the 1981–1982 academic year, interest on these loans was 5%.

An individual can borrow up to $3,000 a year if he or she is enrolled in a vocational program or has completed less than two years of undergraduate study. Students in their third year of undergraduate study may borrow up to a total of $6,000, including any money borrowed during their first two years. For graduate study or professional work, students may borrow up to a total of $12,000, including any amount borrowed under NDSL for undergraduate study.

The student begins to repay the loan six months after graduation or leaving school. Payments can be extended over ten years. The amount of the payment depends on the amount borrowed and how quickly the student wishes to repay the loan.

Auxiliary loans are federally supported loans to parents, graduate students, and some undergraduates who receive no parental support. The repayments must begin within 60 days of receiving the loan. However, they can be spread over a five- or ten-year period.

Parents may borrow up to $3,000 a year, up to a total of $15,000 per undergraduate student. Graduate students may borrow up to $3,000 a year. Independent undergraduate students may borrow up to $2,500 a year. This loan, combined with a guaranteed student loan, may not exceed the annual and total guaranteed student loan limits.

Always compare interest rates and conditions before taking a loan.

Interest on auxiliary loans is higher than on guaranteed student loans. For the 1981–1982 academic year, the rate was 14%. These loans are not yet available in all states. The states must guarantee the loans.

Financial institutions may give education loans. If your child cannot obtain a federally subsidized loan, apply at a local bank, thrift, or credit union. Always compare interest rates and conditions before taking a loan. Rates will vary, and some savings institutions give a more favorable rate to depositors.

College Work-Study Programs exchange financial aid for work. Check the school's financial aid office for application forms. The amount of the award depends on need and the amount of money the school has allocated for this program. The student's work schedule is arranged according to his or her class schedule.

Students are paid at least the federal minimum wage and are limited to earning only the amount of their awards. Undergraduate students are paid by the hour; graduate students may be paid by the hour or receive a salary.

Jobs available under work-study programs may be on or off campus, but all are for nonprofit agencies.

Applying for financial aid

Parents and students are expected to contribute to financing a college education. Even if the parent's income is too low to contribute to the college expenses, the student will be expected to pay some of the costs by working part time or during the summer.

Family income is the basic guideline for determining how much parents can contribute, but the estimate is adjusted for the size of the family and the number of children in college. Any debts, such as a mortgage or other loan, or special expenses, will also lower the estimate. On the other hand, families with substantial assets, such as a large savings account or other investments, will be expected to pay more.

In order to obtain financial aid, the student must apply for it before the school's or program's deadline date. When getting application forms from colleges, request financial aid forms as well. Most colleges require applicants to fill out a Financial Aid Form (FAF) published by the College Scholarship Service. Students may also have to fill out the college's own forms and send a copy of their parents' most recent tax return to verify the information.

The FAF is designed to determine the family's economic position. Its questions concern income, debts, assets, size of family, number of children in college, and age of the parents. Based on this information, it gives a preliminary estimate of how much aid a student can expect and sends him or her an FAF Need Analysis Report. Copies of this report, with copies of the original FAF, are sent to the student's preferred colleges. The College Scholarship Service charges $6.50 for the first college (or scholarship fund, etc.) listed on the FAF and $4.50 for each additional college. Students can also indicate on the FAF that they wish to be considered for federal student aid programs, and information will be forwarded to the federal agencies at no cost.

Cooperative education programs

Hundreds of colleges across the country now offer cooperative education programs, which are work-study programs set up by the schools themselves. In these programs, students take courses and work part time or alternate periods of classes and periods of working. The school usually finds the jobs, frequently in the student's area of study. The student can earn money toward tuition and gain valuable work experience. At community colleges, the program generally runs the usual two years. At four-year colleges, it may take five years to earn a degree while participating in a co-op program.

If your child considers a cooperative college, find out what jobs students are getting through the co-op and what the academic requirements of the program are.

If your child considers a cooperative college, find out what jobs students are getting through the co-op and what the academic requirements of the program are. Ask students or alumni their opinion of the program. Also, find out when your child would begin working. At many four-year schools, students do not begin working until their sophomore year; your child might not mind the wait, but you would have to fit all the costs of the more expensive first year into your financial plans.

For more information on schools offering co-op programs, write to the National Commission for Cooperative Education, 360 Huntington Avenue, Boston, MA 02115.

Information on college costs and financial aid

You will be able to finance a college education with greater ease if you know what aid is available. As early as possible, the student should check the high school guidance counselor's office and local library for information on colleges and financial aid. Also, colleges will mail information to prospective students.

You can send away for a free booklet, "Meeting College Costs: A Guide for Parents and Students," from the College Entrance Examination Board Publications Order Office, Box 2815, Princeton, NJ 08540. This booklet is updated annually.

Don't Miss Out by Robert Leider (published by Octameron Associates) is a regularly updated book on scholarships and loans.

Scholarship search firms will send a computer printout of scholarships for which your child may be eligible. The fees can run to $40 or more, but the information is the same as you can personally obtain by investigating the financial aid options at the schools your child is considering.

Saving for college

With advance planning, you will be able to provide or assist in providing a college education for your children. Below is a table of projected costs for four years of college at different inflation rates.

ESTIMATED COSTS OF A COLLEGE EDUCATION

Current age of child	State universities Inflation rate			Private institutions Inflation rate		
	6%	10%	12%	6%	10%	12%
18	$8,000	$8,000	$8,000	$40,000	$40,000	$40,000
17	8,480	8,800	8,960	42,400	44,000	44,800
16	8,989	9,680	10,035	44,944	48,400	50,076
15	9,528	10,648	11,239	47,641	53,240	56,197
14	10,100	11,713	12,588	50,499	58,564	62,941
13	10,706	12,884	14,099	53,529	64,420	70,494
12	11,348	14,172	15,791	56,741	70,862	78,953
11	12,029	15,589	17,686	60,145	77,948	88,427
10	12,751	17,148	19,808	63,754	85,743	99,038
9	13,516	18,863	22,185	67,579	94,317	110,923
8	14,327	20,749	24,847	71,634	103,749	124,233
7	15,187	22,824	27,829	75,932	114,124	139,141
6	16,098	25,106	31,168	80,488	125,536	155,838
5	17,064	27,617	34,908	85,317	138,090	174,539
4	18,088	30,379	39,097	90,436	151,899	195,484
3	19,173	33,435	43,789	95,862	167,089	218,942
2	20,323	36,778	49,044	101,614	183,798	245,215
1	21,542	40,456	54,929	107,711	202,178	274,641

The estimated cost of college education for your children may be staggering. The best advice, of course, is to start early and save systematically. But, parents do not easily visualize a toddler as a college freshman. Also, there are other financial priorities, such as purchasing a home or business, which overshadow an event so far in the future. Nonetheless, an organized saving plan may be the only way for middle income parents to pay for college. Here are some options:

Savings plans at a bank or other financial institution can be used to build up funds for college. You can use term accounts or money market funds to get higher returns than with passbook accounts. The disadvantage with such savings plans is that you will be taxed on the interest income, thereby reducing the amount accumulated for college expenses.

The best advice, of course, is to start early and save systematically.

Taxes can be lowered and accumulations increased by setting up an account in your child's name, if state banking laws permit, or by creating a custodial account. Your child's income may be so low that no tax will be due on the interest, or if there is a tax, it will be at much lower rates than if it were taxed to you.

Custodial accounts are permitted in all 50 states; you may put cash or securities in an account for your child, with you or someone else named as custodian. The custodian invests the funds until the child reaches majority—age 18 in most states, 21 in some others. Upon reaching majority, the child receives the accumulated funds. The custodial account allows investment flexibility since investments can be switched if market conditions change.

The custodial account is an irrevocable gift to the child. It has income tax advantages because account earnings will be taxed in the child's low tax bracket as long as they are not used for support items, such as food or clothing for the child. You will be taxed if account earnings are used to currently support your child. Another income tax advantage is that although a custodial account may accumulate substantial income, you may still claim a child who is under age 19 or is a full-time student as a dependent. Further, under liberalized gift tax laws, you may make substantial gifts to your child's custodial account without incurring gift tax. Each year, gifts of up to $10,000 may be made to any one person without owing gift tax. Thus if you have three children, you may put up to $10,000 in each child's account each year without owing gift tax. If your spouse consents to gift splitting, you may give up to $20,000 annually to each child's account without having to pay gift tax.

Keep in mind that although a custodial account is a convenient way to accumulate funds for a minor child, it has this drawback: your child will receive the entire account upon reaching majority—either 18 or 21, depending on state law—and may spend the money as he or she chooses. But even if the funds are not ultimately used for college, you may take

---

The custodial account allows investment flexibility since investments can be switched if market conditions change.

---

consolation in having used a custodial account to split income within the family and reduce overall family taxes.

United States Series EE bonds can be purchased by you in your child's name either on your own or where you work if your employer has a bond plan. Taxes on interest may be deferred until the bonds are redeemed by the child, but taxes may be saved by having the child report the interest annually on his or her return. Reporting the interest annually will usually be the better alternative because, if the taxes are deferred, the child would have to pay tax on the accumulated interest when the bonds are redeemed to pay college costs, reducing the amount available for expenses. Savings bonds are discussed in detail in Chapter 2.

Education trusts are short-term or so-called ten-year trusts which can be used to build up an education fund while saving taxes within the family. You may transfer any income-producing property you own to the trustee for investment during the trust term. As long as the trust term lasts at least ten years plus one day, trust income will be taxed to your child rather than to you. An extra advantage of a ten-year trust is that you do not permanently give up your property, you get it back at the end of the trust term.

Here is how the trust could be set up. When your child is seven or eight years old, you set up a trust to last until the child reaches college age, a period of just over ten years. For gift tax purposes, you must provide that the trust's annual income be distributed, either to a custodial account for the child or to a regular bank account in the child's name if permitted by state law, or the trust income may be invested in bonds in the child's name. By providing for such a distribution of trust income, you are able to claim the $10,000 annual gift tax exclusion (or $20,000 if your spouse consents to split the gift) for the value of the child's income interest in the trust. The $10,000/$20,000 exclusion may allow you to avoid gift tax completely. Income from the custodial account or other investments will be taxed to the child during the trust term. When your child is ready to start college, the trust will end and the trust property will be returned to you. Your child will begin to withdraw funds from the account or cash in the bonds to pay college expenses.

An extra advantage of a ten-year trust is that you do not permanently give up your property; you get it back at the end of the trust term.

There is another reason for starting the trust while your child is young rather than waiting until your child is in his or her teens. If the trust is in existence while your child is attending college and your state has a law which legally obligates you to pay for your child's college education, you may face an IRS argument that trust income is being used to discharge your legal support obligation. You instead of your child would then be taxed on the trust income. Check with your attorney to see if there is such a support requirement in your state. Even if your state has a support requirement, it may not apply once your child reaches age 18. If at age 18 your child is considered to be an emancipated adult whom you are no longer required to support, you need not worry about the IRS argument even if your child uses trust income to pay his or her college costs.

Even if you are protected by state law from the IRS's support argument, you may still have a tax problem if the trust pays your child's college bills directly. Do not obligate yourself to pay the expenses when you are discussing admission requirements with the school. For example, in his negotiations with a college one father agreed to be personally liable for the expenses. When his trust paid these bills, the IRS taxed him on the trust income because the trust had discharged his obligation to pay the bills which he had legally assumed. A court agreed with the IRS.

Where the trust is set up while your child is young and it ends at or about the time your child starts college, the IRS cannot argue that trust income is being used to discharge your support obligation. Regardless of what state law says about your obligation to pay college costs or the age of emancipation, you cannot be taxed on the trust income because the trust no longer exists.

State-supported savings plans in some states encourage saving for a college education. For example, New York allows a parent to set up a college fund with a bank. Under the plan, called Parent and Student Savings (PASS) Plan, up to $750 may be contributed each year on behalf of each child. The contribution is deductible for state income tax purposes, as is interest earned on the contributions. The child will be taxed on the money eventually, but presumably he or she will be in a lower tax bracket than the parents were when they made the contribution.

Remortgaging your home is taking a loan, using your home as collateral, to pay college costs. However, this is a major undertaking and should be considered carefully. Assume you bought your home ten years ago. Its value may have doubled, while at the same time you have amortized a portion of your mortgage. Assume your home cost $45,000 with a

$35,000 mortgage for 25 years at 7½%. Your mortgage is now $30,000, but your home is worth $90,000 in today's market. If you remortgaged your home, a bank would probably give you 80% of its value or $72,000. After paying off your first mortgage, you are left with $42,000 which may be enough to put your child through college. With a second mortgage, your monthly payments are considerably higher, but interest can be deducted on your tax return. This deduction will be of greatest benefit to those in higher tax brackets. Also, you have the life of the mortgage, say, 25 years, to pay what is really a college tuition loan and the rate of interest on the mortgage may be less than on a personal loan.

Insurance plans are offered by insurance companies to save for future education costs. One type of plan is an endowment policy taken out on your child at birth, or at a very young age, and is payable in 15 or 20 years. A $10,000, 20-year policy would cost about $450 a year. At the end of the 20-year term, the policy would pay about $15,000 (which includes dividends earned in the policy).

An alternative plan would be to take out a whole-life policy on the parent. That same $450 a year could buy from $40,000 to $50,000 of insurance, depending on the parent's age. At the end of the same 20-year period, the cash value of the policy would be about $13,000. Of course, if the parent died in the interim, the face amount of the policy could have been used to fund an education trust. These insurance plans are costly, but for those who feel they lack the discipline to structure and continue their own savings program, such plans may be a wise alternative.

Chapter 11

PLANNING FOR YOUR RETIREMENT

AMERICANS are living longer. People retiring today at age 65 can look forward to living many happy and fulfilling years which can be enhanced by financial security.

Though retirement may lie many years ahead of you, you would do well to start planning for it early so that the after-65 years are free of the cares that have beset so many retired people due to the inflationary increases in basic living costs.

The projection of living costs on page 204 will show you what you may need to maintain your present standard of living 20 years from now. Apart from what may occur to retirees in the next century, what are prospects today for retirees? If inflation were at only 5% annually, $1,000 set aside in 1982 would have diminished to $614 of purchasing power in ten years. At 7% annual inflation, that $1,000 would buy only about half of 1982's goods and services. These figures make uncomfortable reading. We hope that the projections will prove to be alarmist. Nevertheless, the trend is there: preparation must be made through savings, sound investments, and, where possible, through continued earnings.

INFLATION RATES CONSTANT FOR 20 YEARS

Item	% of Budget	Cost	6%	10%	12%
Housing	20	$2,000	$6,418	$13,457	$19,296
Food	20	2,000	6,418	13,457	19,296
Clothing	15	1,500	4,814	10,093	14,472
Transportation	9	900	2,888	6,056	8,683
Utilities	8	800	2,567	5,383	7,718
Entertainment	8	800	2,567	5,383	7,718
Medical expenses	7	700	2,246	4,710	6,754
Household maintenance	5	500	1,605	3,364	4,824
Savings	5	500	1,605	3,364	4,824
Miscellaneous	3	300	963	2,019	2,894
Total	100	$10,000	$32,091	$67,286	$96,479

Projecting your retirement needs

At retirement, your needs will change; some expenses will diminish while others will increase. Here is a checklist of changes you may expect:

Decreased expenses:

1. Work-related expenses will stop, such as the cost of commuting to and from work and lunches away from home.
2. Payments to retirement plans will end.
3. Federal income taxes will be lower because of lower taxable income, extra personal exemptions for being 65 or over, tax credit for the elderly, and receipt of nontaxable income such as Social Security. However, you may have to budget for estimated tax payments on income from savings and investments.
4. Mortgage payments may be completed. This would occur for example, where you purchased your house at age 40 on a 25-year mortgage. You would own your house outright at age 65.
5. Savings will no longer be a major budgeting factor since retirement is the time to use your hard-saved dollars.
6. You may be entitled to a reduction in property taxes. This break for senior citizens is spreading across the country. Check with your state or county government to see if this benefit is available to you.

7. Your overall living expenses may be less if you move to an area where living costs are lower.

Increased expenses:

1. Medical costs statistically increase with age. Medical insurance, borne by your employer before retirement, will have to be paid by you unless there is a retiree health plan. Medicare covers some of your costs, but you must still pay an ever-increasing yearly deductible and per diem charges if hospitalized for more than 60 days.

2. Recreational expenses may increase because of free time available to pursue travel and hobbies, but these increases cannot be generalized; only you know how you will spend your time.

As a rule of thumb, which must be adapted to your own lifestyle, if your retirement income equals 75% of your preretirement income, your retirement will be comfortable; if your retirement income is only 40% to 50% of preretirement income, you are in for a struggle. Make a realistic projection of your needs, then see if your retirement income will be satisfactory.

What will your retirement income be? Here are usual sources of retirement income: Social Security; pension from employment or union; profit-sharing plan; individual retirement accounts (IRAs); retirement plans for self-employed persons; annuity or other insurance payments; return on investments; interest from savings; rents; royalties; and personal business.

As a rule of thumb, if your retirement income equals 75% of your preretirement income, your retirement will be comfortable.

How many of these income sources will you have when you retire? If you are fairly young, you may not have thought much about the subject. You know you will be entitled to Social Security benefits; you may also be relying on a company pension plan. However, these sources are limited, and the declining power of the dollar over recent decades should warn you that several sources of income should be developed, the earlier the better.

Company pension and profit-sharing plans

If you are an employee covered by a pension or profit-sharing plan maintained by your employer, you should get information about your company plan: the amount of benefits, how they will be paid, and when you will be entitled to them. This information can be obtained from your plan's administrator.

Retirement plans vary. There are defined contribution plans and defined benefit plans. In a defined contribution plan, a contribution is made to an account maintained for you. The amount of the contribution is fixed according to a formula. A profit-sharing plan, which is a type of defined contribution plan, has a formula for allocating profits to the pension fund of each covered employer. The retirement benefits from a defined contribution plan cannot be estimated because they will depend on how much is contributed, how much is earned on the account, and how many years contributions are made. However, each year you can see how large your account has grown. A defined benefit plan provides for specific benefits on retirement and requires that contributions be based on actuarial data to provide the fixed benefit.

The plan may be described as a contributory or noncontributory plan. A contributory plan means that employees contribute to it; a noncontributory plan means that only the employer contributes. Contributing plans have this advantage: income earned on your contributions in your employer's plan is not currently taxed to you. Thus your investment may accumulate without current tax costs. Moreover, your money may grow faster by having expert investors handle it. But be forewarned that you could also lose a portion of it. Your contributions are a form of forced savings. If you have difficulty saving, voluntary contributions to your company plan may be advisable.

When you receive your benefits, your contributions are not taxed. Your own contributions also are not subject to forfeiture, as are vested benefits derived from employer contributions in the case of death before retirement if the plan provides for such forfeitures.

The estimated size of your retirement benefits may be misleading because the actual benefits you will receive are affected by "vesting." Each plan may adopt its own schedule of determining how much of accrued retirement benefits you are entitled to receive, based on how long you have worked for the employer. The law sets maximum vesting schedules to ensure that once you have worked for a minimum time, all your accrued benefits are yours. If you leave your employer, you will not lose your benefits.

When will benefits be paid? Each plan sets its own retirement date, such as age 60 or 65. Further, plans may provide an early retirement date, although opting for early retirement means reduced benefits. Benefits are not generally paid unless you actually retire. However, if you are an owner or a key employee, you must begin to receive benefits at age 70½, whether you retire or not. In some cases, when you leave your job before retirement age, you may be able to receive a distribution of benefits. In this case, you may consider rolling over your benefits to the plan of your new employer or to an IRA. If you do make a rollover to an IRA, you can begin receiving benefits at age 59½ regardless of your employment status.

Each plan may adopt its own schedule of determining how much of accrued retirement benefits you are entitled to receive, based on how long you have worked for the employer.

How will benefits be paid? The plan sets forth the method of payment. Some plans pay a monthly annuity beginning at retirement or use all your benefits to buy an annuity. The annuity may extend for just your life or it may cover the joint lives of you and your spouse. Some plans pay out a lump sum. You may have a choice of how benefits are paid. For income tax purposes, lump-sum distributions receive favorable tax treatment because the law allows you to figure the tax on the distribution using a special ten-year averaging method resulting in a low effective rate of tax on the distribution.

Social Security benefits

Social Security is a government program to provide retired workers and others with retirement funds and other benefits. There has been much publicity on the fiscal stability of Social Security since there will be fewer workers to support more retirees in the coming years. Nevertheless, the program is likely to continue with some changes by Congress. Because the law on Social Security is revised often, you should inquire at a local Social Security office for details of current benefits and requirements.

Generally, the Social Security program provides four types of benefits:

1. Retirement benefits for workers and for spouses and dependent children of retirees. These benefits begin at age 65 or at a reduced level at age 62.
2. Survivor's benefits for the spouse, minor children, and dependent elderly parents of a worker who dies.
3. Disability benefits for a worker who is unable to work for an extended period of time. Benefits are also paid to the spouse and children of a disabled worker.
4. Medical insurance (Medicare) beginning at age 65 and for disabled workers who have been receiving disability payments for at least 24 months.

Qualifying for benefits. You must work for a required period of time in covered employment to obtain an insured status. The required time depends on your age or the date of your retirement, death, or disability. If you have worked for at least ten years in covered employment, you are fully insured, regardless of your age. If you have not, you may still qualify under one of several tests which give insured status even if you have less than ten years in covered employment. There are two types of coverage, currently insured status and fully insured status.

Currently insured status. This protection is designed for the benefit of the families of those who die without having enough coverage to qualify for retirement benefits.

If you are currently insured at the time you die, survivor benefits are payable to:

Your unmarried children (or dependent grandchildren whose parents are dead or disabled), if under 18 or disabled of any age.

Your spouse (or divorced spouse), if caring for your child under 18.

Also payable under the currently insured status are lump-sum death benefits to a spouse or minor child.

Fully insured status. If you have fully insured status, you and your family may receive retirement and disability benefits, and your family also receives protection in case of your death. Retirement benefits are payable to the following:

The insured worker, at age 62 or over.

Spouse, or divorced spouse, 62 or over.

Spouse, any age, if caring for child under 18.

Children or grandchildren (if qualified as above).

In addition, survivor's benefits are paid as under the *currently insured* section, and *fully insured status* may also provide survivor benefits to:

Widow, widower, or divorced spouse, age 60 or over, earlier if disabled.

Dependent parent, 62 or over.

Working wives should note that they have their own earnings record and can collect benefits on their own. They need not wait until their husbands retire to collect benefits.

Students, age 18 to 22, who receive Social Security benefits because a parent is disabled, retired, or deceased, may receive benefits through their college years if they had been receiving benefits and began college by May 1982. However, students' benefits have been reduced and are being phased out; they will end after April 1985.

Keep a record of credits. The Social Security Administration has been criticized for not keeping up with workers' earnings records. Do not risk a problem by ignoring your record. At least once every three years, you should mail Form SSA–

210 SMART MONEY MANAGEMENT

7004, Request for Statement of Earnings, to the Social Security Administration, P.O. Box 56, Baltimore, MD 21203. This form is available at your local Social Security office and the headquarters in Baltimore. You will receive a response in about six weeks.

Social Security forms state that if you wait more than three years, three months, and 15 days after an error is discovered to request a correction, a change may not be possible. The agency waived the deadline in 1981 since it had fallen behind in its record keeping, but you should still try to correct any errors immediately.

If you are age 55 or older, your local Social Security office can give you an estimate of your retirement benefits.

You cannot collect Social Security without applying for it.

Applying for Social Security benefits. You should register at the local Social Security office three months before your 62nd or 65th birthday, depending on which year you plan to retire. This allows enough time for your application to be processed and to locate all necessary information.

You cannot collect Social Security without applying for it. The government is not obligated to remind you of your rights or benefits. You must write to, telephone, or go to your local Social Security office for information and to begin the collection process.

Medicare. When you apply for Social Security benefits at 65, your enrollment in Part A Medicare, covering hospitalization, is automatic. At the same time, you enroll for Part B, covering medical-surgical expenses, for which there is a monthly premium, currently $13.50, which is usually deducted from the monthly Social Security payments. If you do not choose to enroll in Part B in the initial enrollment period (three months before the month in which you turn 65 to three months after that month), you may sign up later, but your premium would be higher than if you enrolled initially.

There is no premium for Medicare Part A, hospital coverage, if you meet Social Security work requirements. If you are not eligible for benefits, you may still obtain Part A Medicare by paying a monthly premium, currently $132. There is a deductible of $304 for the first 60 days of hospitalization. From the 61st to the 90th day, you pay co-insurance of $76 a day. A long-term patient then enters a lifetime reserve of 60 days for which there is a daily charge of $152.

Part A also pays for nursing services (except private-duty nursing), usual drugs and supplies for hospital patients, and other services and treatments furnished by the hospital. A patient transferred to a qualified nursing home after three days of hospitalization pays $38 a day after 20 days in the facility; Part A coverage ends after 100 days. Home health services for patients confined to home are covered by Part A.

If your company has no retiree health insurance coverage to supplement Medicare, you must buy individual policies to help cover the gaps in both Parts A and B.

Part B is for the services of physicians and surgeons and certain medical and health services. It pays 80% of "reasonable charges." The patient is liable for any amounts considered above "reasonable charges," the remaining 20% of costs, and an annual deductible of $75.

The rising costs in the Medicare program which must be borne by the patient weigh heavily on the retiree with diminished income. If your company has no retiree health insurance coverage to supplement Medicare, you must buy individual policies to help cover the gaps in both Parts A and B. As of July 1, 1982, the federal government will certify those so-called medigap policies that meet federal standards. Be sure to obtain approved coverage as many retirees have been victimized in the past by inadequate or unnecessary and high-priced policies. You can obtain a free booklet, "Guide to Health Insurance for People With Medicare," by writing to the Office of Beneficiary Services, Health Care Financing Administration, 648 East Highrise, 6325 Security Boulevard, Baltimore, MD 21207.

212 SMART MONEY MANAGEMENT

Even when you have bought additional insurance to cover gaps in Medicare insurance, you must be prepared to meet costs which are still not covered. Visits to a doctor's office, in particular, have not been covered by supplementary policies though minor surgery may be; the patient often finds the annual Part B deductible, the 20% of costs, and the difference between a doctor's charge and the Medicare payment adds up to a sizable financial responsibility. Though the medicaid program of your state may assist, there have been many cuts in these funds and the income qualifications are becoming even more stringent. In your retirement planning, allocate sufficient funds to cover the possibility of high medical expenses.

Social Security and retirement planning

For many, Social Security is a necessary mainstay of their retirement income. However, Social Security benefits can only cover some basic needs, and thus they should not be the only source of funds in your retirement plans. A substantial savings account, income from investments, and, in some cases, work after retirement should supplement Social Security benefits.

Should you retire early? This is a decision that must take into account your overall financial picture, as well as your personal goals and work opportunities. We consider here only the effect of your decision on Social Security benefits. If you choose to retire early, you may do so and begin to receive

---

A substantial savings account, income from investments, and, in some cases, work after retirement should supplement Social Security benefits.

---

benefits at age 62 (generally in the month following your birthday). However, the amount of your monthly benefits is permanently reduced. The reduction is figured by a formula based on the number of months before age 65 that you retire. If you retire at the earliest age, 62, your monthly benefit is reduced by about 20%. Retiring at age 62 means that if you live until age 77 you will receive more total benefits from the system than if you delay retirement until 65. Age 77 is the break-even point at which it makes no overall difference if you opted for early retirement. Beyond age 77, you receive more benefits overall if you had waited until 65 to retire. For those born after 1937, the full retirement age will increase in gradual monthly stages. The retirement age for those born in the years 1938 through 1942 will be between 65 years, two months, and 65 years, ten months; 66 for those born in the years 1943 through 1954; 67 for those born in 1960 and later. The early retirement age of 62 for reduced benefits has not been changed.

Should you delay retirement? If you do not retire at age 65, you increase the retirement benefit you will receive when you retire. For those born in 1916 or earlier, the increase is 1% per year for each year of delayed retirement; for those born in 1917 or later, the increase is 3% a year. No additional credit accrues in the month you reach 70. The 3% credit will gradually increase starting in 1990 until it reaches 8% in 2009.

What is the effect of working after you begin to receive retirement benefits? If you are 65 or older but under 70, you can earn $6,600 in 1983 without losing benefits. If you are under 65 for the whole year, you can earn $4,920 in 1983 without losing benefits. Once you earn more than these amounts, benefits are reduced. For each $2 you earn, you lose $1 in benefits. A special month rule applies in the year you reach retirement age. Earnings include self-employment income. A more liberal earnings test will apply starting in 1990, when $1 in benefits will be withheld for each $3 of earnings above the annual limit.

For those age 70 or over, benefits are not affected by earnings. Thus you can work, earn any amount, and receive full Social Security benefits.

As long as you continue to work, you pay Social Security taxes on your earnings, regardless of your age.

Benefits may be subject to tax. Starting in 1984, a portion of your Social Security benefits will be subject to tax if the total of 50% of benefits, adjusted gross income and tax-free interest exceeds $25,000 if you are single or $32,000 if you are married and file a joint return. If the $25,000 or $32,000 base is exceeded, up to 50% of benefits may be subject to tax, depending on the amount of your other income.

Retirement savings through IRAs

All working Americans can now benefit from the tax laws designed to encourage retirement savings. Tax-approved retirement plans, such as individual retirement accounts (IRAs) and Keogh plans, offer two main advantages: the opportunity to accumulate large funds for retirement without paying taxes until benefits are withdrawn, and the immediate benefits of deducting your contributions.

The following chart shows how much can be accumulated in an IRA if maximum contributions are made, depending on how long contributions are continued and the rate of interest that is earned.

$2,000* invested annually at	Number of years invested							
	5	10	15	20	25	30	35	40
8%	$11,740	$28,980	$54,300	$91,520	$146,200	$226,580	$344,640	$518,020
10%	12,200	31,880	63,540	114,540	196,700	328,980	542,040	885,180
12%	12,700	35,100	74,560	144,100	266,660	482,660	866,340	1,534,160
15%	13,480	40,600	95,160	204,880	425,580	869,480	1,762,340	3,558,020

* Married couples, where each spouse earns at least $2,000, may double these figures.

What do these accumulations mean for retirement income? Take this example: Say you are now age 50 and make maximum contributions to an IRA earning 12% until you are 65. You would have a fund of about $75,000. If your account continued to earn 12% annually, you could withdraw $10,000 each year for 20 years before the principal is used up. If you had begun contributions at age 40, at age 65 you would have a fund of about $266,000. You would be able to withdraw $33,000 annually for 20 years before exhausting the principal. A million-dollar fund earning 12% allows withdrawals over 20 years of $133,000 each year.

If you are working, you may contribute and deduct up to $2,000 a year. If you work only part time and earn less than $2,000, you may contribute up to 100% of your compensation. Your contribution is tax deductible whether or not you itemize deductions.

Your contribution must be based on payments received for rendering personal services, such as salary, wages, commissions, tips, fees, bonuses, or self-employment earned income.

You do not need special IRS approval to set up an IRA account. Banks, brokerage firms, mutual funds, and insurance companies offering IRA investment plans will provide all the necessary forms.

You may not deduct contributions made in the year you reach age 70½.

You do not need special IRS approval to set up an IRA account. Banks, brokerage firms, mutual funds, and insurance companies offering IRA investment plans will provide all the necessary forms. You may set up your 1982 IRA any time during 1982 or until April 15, 1983 (or later if you have an extension to file your tax return).

You may set up an IRA plan as an *individual retirement account,* using a trust or custodial account with a bank, savings and loan association, federally insured credit union, or other qualified trustee or custodian. While you must begin to receive distributions from the account by the age of 70½, you may provide that your interest will be paid out during the remainder of your life, or the joint life and last survivor expectancy of you and your spouse. If you die before receiving the entire interest in the account, the remaining interest must be distributed to your beneficiaries (or used to purchase an immediate annuity) within five years after death.

You may set up your account following a Treasury model form or model custodial form. If you use this method, you still have to find a bank or other institution or trustee to handle your account or investment. If you manage your own IRA, you may not invest in collectibles. Such an investment is deemed to be a distribution subject to premature withdrawal penalties.

You may also set up your IRA as an *individual retirement annuity* by purchasing an annuity contract (which may include a joint and survivor contract for the benefit of you and your spouse) or an endowment contract issued by an insurance company. No trustee or custodian is required. The contract, endorsed to meet the terms of an IRA, is all that is required. In the case of an endowment contract, however, no deduction is permitted for the portion of the premium allocable to life insurance. Distributions from an endowment policy because of death are taxed as ordinary income to the extent allocable to retirement savings; to the extent allocable to life insurance, they are considered tax-free insurance proceeds.

Instead of setting up your own IRA, you may be able to contribute to your employer's plan if your employer has a qualified plan that permits voluntary contributions. In general, the rules for IRA contributions to employer-sponsored plans are the same as for personal IRAs except that distributions from employer-sponsored plans do *not* have to start at age 70½, as they must with personal IRAs. Rollovers from the employer plan may be made to a personal IRA without incurring any withdrawal penalty, subject to the rule which limits rollovers to one per year.

IRAs for couples. Married couples have an opportunity to increase retirement savings through IRA investments. If you and your spouse work, each may contribute 100% of earnings up to $2,000 in separate IRA accounts. If you are eligible to contribute to an IRA and your spouse does not work, you may also make deductible contributions on behalf of your nonworking spouse. The maximum deductible contribution is 100% of earned income up to $2,250. To claim the deduction, you must file a joint return.

You may have two separate IRAs, one for you and one for your spouse, or a single IRA which has a subaccount for you and another subaccount for your spouse. A joint account is not allowed. However, each spouse may have a right of survivorship in the subaccount of the other. If you already have an IRA for yourself and you want to make contributions on behalf of your nonworking spouse, you may do so by merely opening a new IRA for your spouse while you continue your present IRA for yourself.

If you set up an account (or a subaccount) for your spouse, your spouse must not have any compensation, including tax-exempt foreign-earned income, for the year. Suppose your spouse stopped working on December 31, 1982, and received a final paycheck on January 5, 1983. According to the IRS, you may not make a contribution in 1983 to your spouse's account under the spousal account rules, even if your spouse is not employed at any time during 1983, because your spouse received pay during 1983. On the other hand, your spouse may receive any amount of unearned income, such as interest, dividends, or Social Security benefits, and your contributions for your spouse are deductible.

Equal contributions to each account are not required; you may divide the contribution in any manner you choose as long as the contribution on behalf of either spouse does not exceed $2,000.

If you are divorced, you may not maintain a spousal account for your former spouse.

No deduction for a spousal IRA may be claimed for the year in which either spouse reaches age 70½ or for any year thereafter (although Congress is currently considering a change in this rule). However, if the working spouse is under 70½, that spouse may continue making contributions on his or her own behalf under the regular IRA rules.

If you are divorced, you may not maintain a spousal account for your former spouse. If you contributed to an account on behalf of your nonworking spouse and divorce later in the year, the contribution is an excess contribution subject to penalties. However, your divorced spouse may be able to set up his or her own IRA and base limited contributions on alimony received, as discussed below.

An amount distributed to one spouse may not be rolled over to an IRA account of the other spouse, except in the case of divorce.

A divorced spouse with little or no earnings is allowed a limited deduction for contributions to an IRA established by the former spouse at least five years before the divorce, provided the former spouse contributed to the account in at least three of the five years preceding the divorce. The divorced spouse's deduction is limited to the lesser of (1) $1,125, or (2) compensation plus alimony received. A divorced spouse with earnings above this amount need not rely on these special rules but may make IRA contributions of 100% of earnings up to $2,000.

Restrictions on IRAs. While IRAs offer you tax savings and investment opportunities, there are these restrictions to consider: You may not start withdrawing from the account until you reach age 59½ or become disabled. If you do take money out of the account or even borrow using the account as collateral, you are subject to a penalty tax. Further, you *must* start withdrawing from the account by age 70½ and contributions after age 70½ are not deductible. All distributions from IRAs are fully taxable as ordinary income. Finally, unauthorized contributions and distributions are subject to penalties.

Retirement savings for the self-employed

A self-employed retirement plan (Keogh plan) gives this tax benefit: (1) for 1983, you may deduct contributions up to the lesser of 15% of net self-employment earnings or $15,000; after 1983 contributions of up to the lesser of 25% of earnings or $30,000 may be deducted; (2) income earned on assets held by the plan can accumulate without being subject to tax during the investment period; and (3) on retirement, your tax on distributions may be reduced by special averaging.

In deciding if you should set up a Keogh plan, estimate your returns on a regular investment program at retirement and compare with an estimate of the amount a self-employed retirement plan would provide.

If your comparison is based on a savings plan at a fixed rate of return, there is no question that the Keogh plan will give a greater return because of the tax benefits provided by law. However, you should also consider these points before making your decision:

1. Inclusion of permanent employees with service of at least three years. You must include your employees in your Keogh plan and contribute funds for their retirement ac-

counts. However, your contributions to their accounts are deductible, thus reducing the cost of your contribution. If you have a large payroll, the cost of including your employees may eliminate your tax savings on your account. This possibility must be calculated in each case. The cost of including employees may be balanced by the goodwill and work incentives achieved by providing them with retirement benefits.

2. The amount of cash available for contributions. After meeting both your personal and business expenses, do you have cash to put into the fund? You may meet part of this problem by providing that the plan is to have a variable formula of contributions to meet fluctuations in income.

3. The availability of funds for emergencies. The retirement fund is frozen until you reach a retirement age of 59½, become disabled, or die. In case of financial emergency before that age, your use of the fund may subject you to penalty tax.

Figuring contributions. For 1983, you may contribute and deduct up to 15% of your earned income, or $15,000, whichever is less. For 1983 earned income generally has the same meaning as net earnings from self-employment for self-employment tax purposes. For example, a broker has net commission income of $24,000; his earned income is considered $24,000. For 1983, he may contribute and deduct up to 15% of this amount, or $3,600. Starting in 1984, the maximum deductible contribution will generally increase to the lesser of 25% of earned income or $30,000.

If your 1983 self-employment income is $750 to $5,000 in a taxable year, and your adjusted gross income is $15,000 or less, you may deduct up to $750 in contributions even though this exceeds 15% of earned income. If you earn less than $750, you may deduct contributions up to 100% of your earned income. This rule will not apply after 1983.

In applying the $15,000 gross income test, only the self-employed's income is considered. The test is applied separately for each individual claiming the deduction.

You may take a full business expense deduction for contributions you make for your employees up to the limits applied to regular qualified plans.

Retirement housing options

If you are planning to retire in the near future, you have to decide where you want to live and what lifestyle you wish to pursue. Should you stay in your present home or apartment, or sell it and move? These factors will affect your final decision: family ties, your health, health care facilities, climate, financial position, availability of part-time work, and your age at retirement.

Staying put. If you are like many homeowners reaching retirement age, your present home is yours free and clear. The mortgage has been paid off. However, taxes and maintenance of your home may still be costly. If you decide you want to stay in your home, will you be able to afford its upkeep and taxes over the next 15 to 20 years? Perhaps your income from Social Security, pension plan, and other investments will cover your living costs adequately. But if you are worried about cash for major repairs, increasing taxes, or emergencies, there may be an alternative to selling your house and moving away. "Equity poor" senior citizens may be eligible for a number of innovations which let them use the equity in their homes to pay bills. These are known as "equity conversion" plans.

In some states, senior citizens can postpone property tax payments. When the house is sold or the owners die, the state collects the taxes due, plus interest on the amount that was deferred. Other states offer home repair loans to older homeowners whose income falls within specified low limits. The loans do not have to be repaid until the house is sold. In another state, senior homeowners can get long-term financing if they want to convert a part of their home to a rental unit or build an addition to rent.

Another way to benefit from the value of your home while staying in it is to take out a reverse annuity mortgage (RAM). With this kind of loan, a homeowner can borrow up to a specified percentage of the value of his house and receive monthly payments from the bank. The homeowner pays interest monthly on the borrowed amount; principal is repaid when the house is sold, or the bank collects from the estate of the owner when he or she dies. RAMs have been available since 1979, but because they are unprofitable only a few banking institutions in the country currently offer them.

Other equity conversion plans are experimental and are also not generally available throughout the country. One plan in use in the San Francisco area is a sale–leaseback in which an investor buys the home of a senior citizen at a discount from the appraised market value, but the elderly seller is allowed to live in the home for life and pay a controlled monthly rent. The amount of the discount depends on the seller's age. The seller receives a percentage of the sale price (usually 10%) immediately; the balance of the purchase price, plus interest, is paid to the seller in monthly installments over 10 or 15 years. In addition, the investor buys the retiree a lifetime annuity to start after the purchase price is paid so that monthly income does not stop. If the seller dies before the mortgage is paid, the balance is paid to the seller's estate. The investor pays the maintenance and insurance costs, as well as the taxes, and can depreciate the investment. The seller pays rent which cannot exceed 50% of the payment received monthly from the buyer. Investors can profit doubly from this kind of investment: first, by purchasing at a discount from market value; second, from the tax write-offs from real estate ownership.

More types of home equity coversion plans are being offered by various organizations. Check in your area for plans that you may be able to take advantage of.

If you are over 55 years old and sell your home at a profit, you may avoid tax on profits up to $125,000.

Selling your home and moving. If you are over 55 years old and sell your home at a profit, you may avoid tax on profits up to $125,000. If your profits are invested for a high fixed return, you will be able to pay rent on a comfortable apartment while also providing an income. For example, if you sell the home you own outright for $100,000 and invest the proceeds for a 10% return, you will have $10,000 annually with which to pay rent and other expenses.

To claim this once-in-a-lifetime exclusion, you must (1) elect to avoid tax; (2) be 55 or over before the date of sale; and (3) have owned and occupied the house as your principal residence for at least three of the five years before the date of sale. This election applies also to cooperative apartment ownership and to condominiums.

If you are planning to buy a new home, be it a house, condo, mobile home, co-op apartment, or even a houseboat, you can defer tax on the gain from the sale of your old house. To qualify, you must buy or build a new home within two years before or after the sale at a cost equal to or exceeding the selling price of your old house. An investment in a retirement home project does not qualify if you do not receive an equity interest in the project. Both the old and the new home must be your principal residence. If you plan to make a rented apartment your principal residence and buy a summer home, you cannot defer gain. Of course, you may make the once-in-a-lifetime exclusion election already discussed.

Retirement community. Not long ago, retirement communities were confined to the Sunbelt. More recently, construction has expanded to every state and is spreading because builders are confident of making a profit. The market is there: by the end of the 1980s, the number of Americans older than 60 will have increased to about 40.2 million and only 10% to 15% of retirees move a great distance from their home at retirement age.

These communities offer a choice of housing. You can buy an apartment, from one room to a two- or three-bedroom unit, a small house, or a house with two or three bedrooms, depending on the selection at each development. Retirement communities always have an age restriction and a ban on small children permanently residing there. Amenities include clubhouse, party rooms, swimming pool, golf course, bike paths, nature walks, gardens, entertainment, arts-and-crafts areas, and organized activities.

Mobile or manufactured homes. Today's mobile home parks are generally clean, well-organized enclaves of manufactured homes often on natural or man-made waterfront sites. It is not unusual for the home to have two to three bedrooms, living room, dining room, full kitchen, sunporch, two baths, car port, and storage shed. Actually, mobile homes are rarely mobile anymore. They are produced on a factory assembly line, delivered to the site in sections, and then permanently affixed to a site. The basic mobile home is a single-wide section from 8 to 14 feet wide and from 40 to 80 feet long. Two or more single-wides can be joined for double- and triple-wides with as much living space as a custom-built home. Multisection units can cost as much as $50,000, but you would spend much more for a conventional home with comparable living space and features. The average price of a mobile home, exclusive of the land, is about $20,000.

Mobile home parks can be quite luxurious, with paved streets, sidewalks, swimming pools, recreation centers, shuffleboard courts, bike-rental facilities, and boating. Most are reasonably priced and offer a relaxed atmosphere and small-town feeling of friendliness.

Before committing yourself to one mobile home community, ask about lease terms, entrance and exit fees, facilities and extra charges, water supply, eviction practices, rules governing children, pets, gardens, fences, shrubbery, and noise. Many parks have an active tenants' group; speak to an officer or member.

If you are ordering a new home, choose a dealer with the utmost care; any problems that develop will be up to the dealer to solve. Check out your prospective dealer with the Better Business Bureau and consumer protection agencies.

Buy a camper and travel. If you have had a yen to travel during your working years but have had to postpone taking trips, you may be able to do it now. Many retirees buy or rent a camper—a mini-home on wheels—and take to the highways for a time before settling down in one place. If you are not sure where you want to settle permanently, traveling around the country is a good way of becoming familiar with different areas and climates. When you cease your wanderings, your camper can be sold to a dealer or sold privately.

Before buying the camper of your choice, figure whether it is better financially to rent it. Check with a number of dealers to determine estimated depreciation for a period or number of miles you plan to keep or use your camper. Then find out what it costs to rent or lease the same camper on a monthly basis. Choose the most economical way after taking into consideration costs for insurance and maintenance.

Buy a smaller home or condominium. Another housing option is simply to buy a small home or condo in an area which offers you the lifestyle you desire. A "community" feeling, such as you would find in a retirement village or mobile home park, may not be for you. Perhaps you prefer to settle in a conventional residential area, especially if you already have friends or family in the vicinity.

Will you have the energy or desire to maintain a house of your own? Do you enjoy yardwork or is it a burden? Will you have the cash to handle repairs and emergencies which may occur? Perhaps buying a condominium is a better choice for you. You own your apartment or town house, but the commons areas are owned and maintained by management so that you are free of most homeowner's tasks.

Share a home. For single retirees, the prospect of sharing a home may be appealing. You can rent out a room in your house or seek a similar arrangement in the home of another retiree. There are also more structured sharing arrangements. For example, you may rent a room and bath in a large home which was purchased by a local civic group through donations or loans. Kitchen facilities are usually not included; shared dining is the norm. Often there are minimal health care facilities on the premises. Your rent includes all operating costs, including those of a housekeeper who cooks and does domestic chores. In this way, residents are free of all housekeeping responsibilities and can come and go as they please. There is the primary advantage of having the company of other residents, combined with the privacy of one's own room. This type of housing arrangement is especially attractive to elderly retired people who are alone and who can adapt to a group living situation.

Where should you retire? Generally, the most popular retirement states are in the Southeast and the Southwest. Warm climate is an obvious attraction; low taxes, cost-of-living advantages, and availability of housing, medical care, and public services are others. According to a Chase Econometrics report, the ten best states in which to retire, based on the above factors, are: Utah, Louisiana, South Carolina, Nevada, Texas, New Mexico, Alabama, Arizona, Florida, and Georgia.

Chapter 12

PLANNING YOUR ESTATE

MANY people delay making a will. Although no one wants to think of dying, it is foolhardy not to plan ahead for your family's welfare. With a will, you can distribute your property as you wish, leave something personal to a friend or relative, choose the executor of your estate, and, in case it

---

Everyone who owns property should make a will.

---

should be necessary, choose a guardian for your minor children. If you die intestate (without a will), the state divides your property according to law, which may give property to someone you would not have included.

Making a will

Everyone who owns property should make a will. Even nonworking wives should make their own wills to distribute any assets and personal items they own. In addition, most wives inherit the bulk of their husbands' estates and must arrange for the distribution of that property.

You should have a lawyer prepare your will. Fees for drawing wills are not high; an average cost is $200, but a complex will costs more. Fees at legal clinics are generally lower. Do not try to save money by drawing a will yourself. If the document is not legally correct, it will be invalid.

List your beneficiaries. Your first step is to write down the names of your immediate family, your spouse, your children (and their ages), your brothers and sisters, your parents. List other beneficiaries you may wish to remember such as a long-time friend, employees, your place of worship, your college, a medical, educational, or other philanthropic organization.

Many charitable organizations have similar names. Be sure that the correct titles appear in your will. If you misname a charitable beneficiary, its identity may have to be decided by a court and the legal expenses involved will be a charge against your estate. List alternative charities in case those you name cease to function or cannot take your bequest.

List your assets. Here, your review of your net worth and your household inventory will help you. Be sure that you have not overlooked a bank account or a bond bought many years ago. This is a common occurrence. Each year, banks and other financial institutions list names of persons who have forgotten their accounts. You might also forget small jewelry or heirlooms, a valuable collection of stamps or coins laid aside years ago.

When you list properties, be sure they are really yours to give.

What about shares of stock purchased long ago and put away? An investment or property not producing income now may seem of little value, but in time it may become valuable. A business that you consider a sideline may become an asset.

When you list properties, be sure they are really yours to give. Note that title to certain properties passes outside your will. Examples of property you cannot bequeath or devise are property held with your spouse either as joint tenants or as tenants by the entirety; insurance payable to a named beneficiary, even though for tax purposes it may be part of your gross estate; United States Savings Bonds held in your name but payable to another at your death; estates in which you had a life interest, but after your death the remainder goes to another.

Describe property in detail. Also give instructions for property in case the heir cannot or will not accept it. In distributing the cash of your estate, use percentages instead of dollar figures. If the amount has changed since you wrote the will, percentages will more accurately reflect your intentions.

Do you have two residences, say, one in New York, the other in Florida? If so, list your possessions in each of the two states so your attorney can draw your will in accordance with the laws of the state in which the will must be probated. Generally, dispositions of personal property are controlled by laws of the state of your principal residence; real property, according to the laws of the state in which it is located. The laws of one state may be more beneficial for your estate than the other. Ask your attorney now what steps you can take to ensure that the disposition of your estate will be made in accordance with the laws of the state which gives the best treatment.

In making a will, your marital status must be considered. Some states, in certain circumstances, allow a surviving spouse to elect to take the share of a deceased spouse's estate under the laws of intestacy in place of the bequest left under a will. In many states, the law protects the rights of adopted children and after-born children not named in a will to share in a parent's estate.

Your state's laws may provide a widow or children with homestead rights or give a widow the right to remain in the family home for a certain length of time with a sustenance allowance from the husband's estate. If the laws of dower or courtesy are in force, they, too, limit the right of disposition over property. In most community-property states (Arizona, California, Idaho, Louisiana, Nevada, New Mexico, Texas, and Washington), each spouse is limited in the portion of property that can be left by will to others.

There should be provision covering the possibility of death of both spouses in, for example, a plane or automobile crash. Your will could provide that if you and your spouse die in a common disaster under circumstances that make it doubtful which died first, it should be presumed for purposes of the will that your spouse survived. Such a provision could save the marital deduction.

Most states require that two people witness the signing of a will, but some states require three witnesses. Having the third

---

There should be provision covering the possibility of death of both spouses in, for example, a plane or automobile crash.

---

witness is a good idea if you own property in a state that requires three witnesses. The witnesses should *not* be beneficiaries under the will.

Your executor

If you do not leave a will, the court will appoint someone to administer your estate. The court's appointee may not be acquainted with your family or sympathetic to their interests. With a will, you can select the person or persons you feel qualified to administer your estate. You may appoint your spouse, an adult child, or both to serve jointly as executors.

If the administration of your estate requires business or professional training and experience, consider appointing an attorney or a business associate as executor. It is possible that the person you name will become unable to perform as an executor. You may provide alternative names.

The executor may serve without bond if you so stipulate. This is usually the case when you name a member of your family as your executor.

Your executor is entitled to commissions for his or her services, generally computed on a percentage basis of the value of all your property and income that passes through the estate. The amount received is a deductible expense in computing your taxable estate. Commissions are fixed by local law, but you can provide in your will that your executor is to act without compensation or that there should be a specified allowance in place of statutory commissions. Your attorney can advise you how to handle your executor's commissions.

Guardians for your children

If in your will you leave property to a minor, name a guardian of the child's property. If you do not, the court will appoint one. Although a parent is considered the natural guardian of the person of a minor, the parent is not the guardian of the child's property unless so named. If you name your spouse as guardian of your child's property, provide an alternate in case he or she dies, or does not qualify to act. The duty of a guardian of property is to hold, manage, and conserve the property for the minor until he or she reaches the age of majority, which varies from state to state. You can name one guardian, or two or more persons to act jointly in this capacity.

Letter of last instruction

In addition to making a will, you should give your lawyer and a family member a letter of last instruction which states the location of your will and other important documents, and lists assets, how they are owned, and their locations. This letter can also give your family instructions for funeral and burial or cremation and inform them whether you already own a cemetery plot or have prepaid any funeral expenses. If your family is entitled to any benefits from your job when you die, give instructions for claiming them. The letter can also leave instructions for running a family business.

Review your will

Review your will periodically, especially when these events occur: your family relationships change; you marry, separate, are divorced; your spouse dies; a child is born, dies, or is adopted; a grandchild is born, dies, or is adopted; your executor dies; your estate increases or decreases substantially; you acquire property in another state or abroad; you move to another state; you retire; inheritance and estate tax laws are changed.

Some changes in your will may only require a codicil; others may require a new will entirely. When executing a codicil, remember that it must, like your will, be legally drawn and witnessed. Any handwritten or typed changes in your will or codicil will invalidate it. When you make a new will, follow your attorney's instructions on how to destroy the old one and any codicils to it.

Safeguarding a will

A common mistake is to store a will in a safe deposit box. In most states, the bank seals the box as soon as it learns of the owner's death. You should ask your lawyer to store your will; keep only a *copy* in a safe place at home. Let a family member know where it is and include this information if you leave a letter of last instruction. If your executor is a bank or trust company, your will can be stored there.

Using a trust to avoid probate

Probate is the court proceeding under which a will is reviewed and property left under the will is distributed to heirs. A probate court may go by the name of surrogate, chancery, or orphan's court, and if your will is contested by disgruntled heirs or creditors, the court will hear and rule on their claims. The court will also interpret any part of your will that is unclear.

You should ask your lawyer to store your will; keep only a copy in a safe place at home.

If you die without a will and your estate is distributed to persons named by intestate laws, a probate court will appoint an administrator of your estate.

Reasons for avoiding probate. Probate proceedings take

time, are expensive, and are open to publicity. The probate of a moderate and uncomplicated estate may take less than six months. Some states have special procedures for expediting the probate of smaller estates. But often complications and the size of an estate can require a probate of two to five years and even longer. During this time, except for certain widow's allowances, the distribution of assets may be delayed.

Reporters usually review the proceedings of probate courts, so it is not unusual for local papers to publicize the estates of area residents, especially where there are disputes or considerable assets. Besides invading privacy, publicity may attract con artists.

Probate requires the payment of attorneys' fees, court costs, and commissions to the executor or administrator. On even a small estate, the cost of probate can be substantial.

Avoiding probate. Probate can be avoided by taking title to property in the form of joint tenancy. Title to the property is simply put into two names, jointly, with a right of survivorship. On the death of the first to die, title immediately passes to the surviving owner without expense, delay, or legal entanglements. The survivor has the right to immediate possession and control of the property.

The advantages of joint tenancy should not blind you to possible drawbacks. Joint tenancy may not adequately meet all the eventualities that take place after death. Jointly owned property may pass to people you did not intend to have the property. Take this example: A childless couple put all their property in joint names. The husband died in an automobile accident that left the wife seriously injured. A few weeks later, she, too, died. Because she was sole owner of the property after her husband's death, all of it went to her brothers and sisters. Her husband's parents received nothing. Had there been no joint tenancy, the husband and wife, through their separate wills, would have been able to distribute individually owned property fairly between both families.

There are other drawbacks. Under state law, the executor or administrator of the estate may not have the power to use jointly held property to pay the taxes or debts of the deceased person. Without this power, other estate assets may have to be sold to raise needed cash, perhaps at sacrifice prices, to satisfy obligations. The survivor may not be able to withdraw funds from a joint bank account until the estate is probated. There are income tax disadvantages to a surviving spouse of a joint tenancy. Finally, unexpected gift tax liability may be incurred in setting up joint tenancy, or on the sale or other disposition of the property.

There are property interests that you may not want to place in joint ownership. You can still avoid probate on such property by putting the property in trust for your intended beneficiaries. The interests of trust beneficiaries are generally more secure than those of heirs under a will. A will may be denied probate if found invalid, and the estate will pass under the state's law of intestacy.

Putting the property in trust does not mean that you must give up control of the property. You can make yourself trustee and the lifetime beneficiary, and keep the power to revoke the trust at any time. Such a revocable trust is not subject to gift tax because you have not made a completed gift. But the trust property is included in your estate for tax purposes and may be subject to tax even though it is not part of your probate estate.

After setting up revocable trusts, you must be careful to follow legal formalities. A revocable trust in which you are both trustee and beneficiary may be held to be a "paper transfer." To provide a basis for treating the transfer as a trust, it is suggested that you: (1) keep the documents of trust ownership in a separate safe deposit box rented by you in your name as trustee; (2) keep a trustee bank account in which all the trust income and other receipts are first deposited; (3) maintain a set of books of all trust transactions; (4) register the assets in your name as trustee; (5) file federal and state fiduciary income tax returns even if you are not taxable on the trust income.

To avoid having the trust included in your estate at its value on your death, you must create an irrevocable trust in which you have not retained any rights. If you retain a lifetime interest in the income or property or the right to designate those who will receive the income or property, the value of the trust property will be included in your gross estate. Similarly, if you retain any power to alter, amend, revoke, or terminate the trust, the property will be included in your estate.

If you are interested in setting up a trust, discuss your plans with your lawyer. The trust department of your bank will also provide information.

Estate tax planning

Under new estate tax laws, it is estimated that by 1987, 99.7% of all estates may be exempt from federal estate tax. However, even if you own sufficient property to subject your estate to tax, you have an opportunity to conserve what you have accumulated. By advance planning, all or substantial amounts of the tax may be avoided.

Legally, the estate tax is a tax on the transfer of property on a person's death. For practical purposes, you may consider it a potential tax imposed on the market value of your property at the date of your death (or six months later, if your executor elects to value property at this date).

Liberal credits and deductions, and above all, planning opportunities, generally help to avoid or lessen the estate tax liability.

Estate tax rates are graduated. The rates start at a low of 18% for the first $10,000 of the taxable estate to a high of 70% on estates exceeding $5 million. Starting in 1982, the top estate tax rate will drop to 65%, 60% in 1983, 55% in 1984, and 50% in 1985. The 50% rate in 1985 will apply to taxable estates over $2.5 million.

Liberal credits and deductions, and above all, planning opportunities, generally help to avoid or lessen the estate tax liability. Each estate is given a unified credit which effectively exempts all or a portion of an otherwise taxable estate. The new law raises this credit over the next six years.

For tax purposes, an understanding of the word "estate" is fundamental. Otherwise, you may underestimate. Generally, any property you own or have an interest in when you die is part of your gross estate. It includes real estate, securities, bank accounts, and personal property, such as jewelry and art objects. It may also include property you own jointly with another person even though you have no right to decide who gets it after you die. Certain property you gave away in the last three years of your life, such as a life insurance policy, may also be part of your estate.

You cannot plan your estate unless you take inventory of everything you own, as well as your debts and liabilities. Debts, of course, reduce your net worth and your estate.

Listing property takes thought, time, and a surprising amount of work with lists, records of purchase, fire and theft insurance inventories, bankbooks, and brokers' statements. You need to include your cash, real estate (here and abroad), securities, mortgages, rights in property, trust accounts, life insurance payable to your estate or payable to others if you have kept a certain measure of ownership, personal effects, collections, and works of art.

**You cannot plan your estate unless you take inventory
of everything you own, as well as your debts and
liabilities.**

If you own property, such as your home, jointly with your spouse, list one-half of its value.

If you have had appraisals made of unusual or specially treasured items or those of substantial value, file them with your estate papers and enter the value in your inventory.

There are assets that you might not ordinarily consider part of your taxable estate. You must include any trust arrangement in which you have retained: (1) life estate (the income or other use of property for life); (2) income which is to be used to pay your legal obligations (support of a child, for example); (3) the right to change the beneficiary or his interest (a power of appointment); (4) the right to revoke or alter the trust transfer or gift; or (5) a reversionary interest (possibility that the property can come back to you).

Also included in your estate are benefits from any of the following retirement plans which are payable to your estate: pension plan; profit-sharing plan; Keogh plan; or individual retirement account. Benefits from any of these plans, which are payable to a beneficiary other than your estate and are not payable in a lump sum, are generally excluded up to $100,000, except to the extent of your own nondeductible contributions to the plan.

How to estimate your taxable estate

The following discussion shows how to arrive at your taxable estate.

Gross estate. This is the total value of all property subject to estate tax at death. Thus, for purposes of estimating the size of your estate, figure the current value of all the property you first included in your inventory. The executor or administrator of an estate may choose to value a decedent's property as of the date of death or at an alternative valuation date. The alternative date is usually six months after death unless assets were sold before six months. In that case, the date of sale is the alternative valuation date.

Adjusted gross estate. This is the gross estate reduced by all deductions discussed below except the marital deduction. The adjusted gross estate is used to determine qualification for estate tax deferral and stock redemptions to pay estate taxes.

Taxable estate. The taxable estate is the adjusted gross estate reduced by the marital deduction.

Deductions. Deductions come under four main categories: (1) expenses and debts; (2) losses during administration; (3) charitable bequests; and (4) marital deduction.

Expenses and debts. Funeral expenses, such as undertaker's charges, cost of burial lot, tombstone, monument, or mausoleum are deductible.

Administration expenses, such as attorneys' fees, executor's or administrator's commissions and expenses, court costs, surrogate fees, and appraisers' fees are also deductible. The fees of trustees are not deductible. If administration expenses have not yet been paid when a return is filed, they can be estimated. For your estimates and planning, figure between 5% and 10% of your estate as an administrative expense.

Personal debts of the deceased that the estate must pay are deductible. These may include interest accrued up to the time of the decedent's death and his unpaid taxes, including income taxes due on earnings up to the time of death. Taxes due on income earned by the estate after the date of death are not deductible in computing the gross estate.

Mortgages and liens on property included in the gross estate are deductible.

Losses during administration. Certain losses which are incurred by the estate during the period of administration are deductible. These are casualty and theft losses which are not compensated for by insurance and not deducted on an income tax return. Losses of this type cannot be predicted or estimated.

Marital deduction. The value of property left a surviving spouse may be deducted. You may give a spouse an unlimited amount of property without any estate tax liability as a result of an unlimited marital deduction. This rule also applies to transfers of community property between spouses.

Only certain property passing to a surviving spouse qualifies for the deduction. This will be discussed later.

Qualified charitable bequests are deductible without limitation.

Credits reduce estate tax

Unified tax credit. Every estate is entitled to a credit which may eliminate or substantially reduce estate taxes by exempting from tax the following:

Year	Credit	Tax-free estates
1982	$62,800	$225,000
1983	79,300	275,000
1984	96,300	325,000
1985	121,800	400,000
1986	155,800	500,000
1987 and thereafter	192,800	600,000

State death tax credit. State death taxes are credited against the federal estate tax. Most states impose death taxes that are at least equal to the maximum credit allowed. The credit is computed on the taxable estate reduced by $60,000. Note that the unified tax credit is deducted from the tentative estate tax before applying the state death tax credit.

Credit for federal estate tax on prior transfers. It sometimes happens that part of the property in an estate was taxed in another estate. Federal estate tax credit is provided to save the second estate from paying full tax again on such property. To get the benefit of this credit, the property must have been included in a taxable estate within ten years before or two

---

If your estate is large enough to be taxed, your attorney may suggest ways to reduce the tax liability.

---

years after the death of the person in question. The amount of the credit is in proportion to the time lapse between the date the property was previously taxed and the date of death of the person whose estate is claiming the credit.

Basic estate planning goals

Estate planners generally direct their plans to these basic goals: (1) reducing or eliminating a potential estate tax; (2) shrinking estate values and providing the means of raising funds to pay a potential estate tax; and (3) anticipating and solving valuation problems that may arise when an estate tax return is prepared.

If your estate is large enough to be taxed, your attorney may suggest ways to reduce the tax liability. There are two general approaches that may be taken to eliminate or reduce a potential estate tax: (1) You may make lifetime gifts that reduce your estate while you are alive. You may give up to $10,000 a year tax free to as many individuals as you like. If you are married and your spouse consents to the gift, you may give up to $20,000 a year to an individual. Also tax free are gifts to charities, gifts to pay school tuition or medical costs, and gifts to your spouse. (2) You may take advantage of laws that remove from the taxable estate assets that might otherwise be taxed. This requires planning property distributions that qualify for the marital deduction, investments in insurance policies that are free from estate tax, and bequests to charitable organizations that qualify for the charitable deduction.

The marital deduction

The tax on an estate can be greatly reduced or even eliminated by the marital deduction. The law allows an unlimited marital deduction for most property passing to a surviving spouse. To qualify, a husband or wife must generally leave the surviving spouse complete and unrestricted ownership of property or must leave the property under an arrangement that is equivalent to complete ownership and which will qualify for the marital deduction. The law permits a deduction for certain life-income interests as well.

If you believe your spouse does not have the experience or desire to manage property, you may not want to give him or her complete and personal control or substantial assets. The law permits a spouse to give the property in trusts that are

---

The law allows an unlimited marital deduction for most property passing to a surviving spouse.

---

considered equivalent to complete ownership. Further, you may leave your spouse an income interest in trust that may qualify for the deduction while your will names the party who is to take the trust property on your spouse's death. If you leave such a qualifying terminable interest property (QTIP), your executor makes an election to treat the interest as property qualifying for the marital deduction under the condition that it is subject to estate tax in the surviving spouse's estate. Tax allocated to the QTIP property is payable out of that property, unless the will of the surviving spouse directs otherwise.

⌐⌐ The J. K. Lasser Tax Institute carries on the tax, financial, and business publications of J. K. Lasser. The Institute under the direction of Bernard Greisman continues the J. K. Lasser tradition of explaining complicated and technical material in terms understandable by the layman. It is also noted for its special tax services for professionals. The most widely read work for the public by the Institute is J. K. Lasser's Your Income Tax which has helped over 23 million taxpayers reduce taxes and make informed financial decisions.